SACRIFICES
FOR
PATRIOTISM

Sacrifices
for
Patriotism

A Korean POW Remembers the Forgotten War

HELEN GREENE LEIGH

BALBOA.
PRESS

A DIVISION OF HAY HOUSE

Balboa Press books may be ordered through booksellers or by contacting:

Balboa Press
A Division of Hay House
1663 Liberty Drive
Bloomington, IN 47403
www.balboapress.com
1-(877) 407-4847

Library of Congress Control Number: 2012917745

ISBN: 978-1-4525-5605-5 (sc)
ISBN: 978-1-4525-5606-2 (hc)
ISBN: 978-1-4525-5604-8 (e)

Printed in the United States of America

Balboa Press rev. date: 10/25/2012

Dedication

—♒︎—

This book has been a labor of love and is dedicated first to my hero, my brother Pharis. I thought when I called him a hero, I knew why but I knew very little until I started doing the research for this book and listening to him recall his experiences as a prisoner of war. His bravery and his will to survive are truly an inspiration and should be admired by everyone. I am honored to be able to write his story and even more honored that I am his sister.

This book is dedicated to all those brave people who served in Korea, both military and civilians, and their families. All of them were heroes and deserve to have their stories told.

This book is dedicated to the others in our family who made sacrifices and suffered with Pharis while he was being held by the Communists. While their pain was not physical, it was certainly emotional. Knowing that someone you love is alone and suffering, without being able to help, is a type of pain that cannot be described.

Father,

Harlan Vue Greene April 29, 1907 – June 22, 1970

Mother,

Maebelle Dobbins Greene March 22, 1913 – September 3, 2004

Sister,

Margaret Greene Wright January 1, 1935 – February 10, 2008

Brother,

Billy Harlan Greene December 8, 1936 – January 8, 2007

Brother,

Chalmers Buren (C. B.) Greene March 11, 1943 – March 9, 2001

PFC Pharis L. Greene

Contents

Prologue

—◊◊◊—

Just 25 days after the North Koreans invaded South Korea on June 25, 1950, they had our 11,700 troops surrounded in Taejon, South Korea. They had us severely outnumbered and there was no way out. Each time our soldiers tried to push out, to punch a hole in the enemy lines, they were faced with 70,000 to 90,000 North Koreans equipped with at least 50 Russian T-34 tanks. Tough decisions had to be made, and Major General William Dean was the one who had to make them.

Dean ordered the men to get everything ready to fight their way out through the enemy lines. They had no other choice. Everything was gassed and greased and lined up in preparation to leave. The wounded men and as many weapons as possible were loaded on the backs of trucks to transport out. Until the time was right and the orders were given to move, our troops waited, in 100 degrees weather. There was no place to go until the time was right.

On July 20, 1950, Dean's orders finally came: move out, try to break through the enemy lines. God be with all of them. Pharis and a few other soldiers jumped into the back of a truck which was carrying seven or eight wounded men. As their truck progressed toward the enemy lines, they braced themselves for the fight of their lives.

Suddenly Pharis' eyes caught a glimpse of a bright light, a flare, coming at his truck. He knew that this could only mean big trouble. He tried to jump from the truck but there just wasn't enough time. An enemy's bazooka shot his driver and blasted all the others out of the back of the truck.

Totally stunned by the blast, Pharis tried desperately to get his bearings. His helmet and rifle has been blown away and Pharis' survivor instincts told him that finding these had to be his first priority. Without these essentials, he had no defense against the enemy. He frantically searched as he crawled low to the ground until he finally laid his hands on both. He then realized that he had been riddled with shrapnel by the blast. He was bleeding profusely where the shrapnel had pierced his skin. The larger pieces had lodged in his left elbow and his right knee. He knew he had to treat these areas to prevent infection. Gangrene could claim his limbs, even his life. Maybe later. Right now he had to hide from the enemy. If they found him, he would most likely be shot again. He might not be as lucky the next time. The next shot could be fatal.

Pharis managed to crawl to a nearby irrigation ditch where he hoped the enemy wouldn't find him. Feeling somewhat safer behind the banks of the ditch, he took a few moments to tend to his wounds. He sprinkled the medical powder supplied by the Army on the bloody spots. Hopefully this powder would prevent infection; he could have the shrapnel surgically removed later. Pharis remained hidden in the ditch until he thought it was safe to keep moving. Maybe he could meet up with some of the other soldiers. As soon as he stood, he discovered that leaches, three inches and longer, had attached themselves to him. He was completely covered from his feet up to his knees. He tried desperately to remove the slimy pests but pulling them from his skin proved to be a very painful process. As they reluctantly turned loose, they left behind gaping holes where they had settled in expecting a long ride.

Pharis finally met up with seven other guys who were also trying to escape the enemy. As he surveyed the situation, he noticed that he was the only one who had retrieved his rifle. Not good. They all scurried around trying to find a proper hiding place, anywhere that they could be invisible to the enemy. They crawled through the infectious rice paddies that had been fertilized with human waste, any place to hide from the barbaric North Koreans.

All too soon, Pharis saw another flare. This time the enemy was using flares to light up the area to determine the exact location of our men. Once the enemy spotted Pharis and the others, they immediately started firing. They shot directly at Pharis and he should have died right then, but the bullet hit the rifle that Pharis had desperately retrieved and knocked it out of his hands. The bullet hit so hard that the impact caused Pharis' hands and arms, all the way up to his shoulders, to remain numb for several hours afterwards. The fact that the bullet hit his rifle and did not penetrate his body was the first of many miracles he would experience during his stay in Korea. He had literally "dodged a bullet" that day.

Some of the guys with Pharis were not as lucky. One soldier was shot in the back of the neck at such an angle that the bullet went down beside his spine, but he could still walk. Another soldier was shot in the gut but could still walk as long as he held his gut in. These guys were surrounded by the enemy; there was no place left to run. These eight soldiers were now the property of the North Korean military and all of them were terrified of what might happen to them next.

Winston Churchill was quoted as saying about the captivity of a prisoner, "You are in the power of the enemy. You owe your life to his humanity, your daily bread to his compassion. You must obey his orders...."

Pharis and the other soldiers had heard the stories about the treatment the North Koreans dished out to anyone they captured. The Communists proved ruthlessly indifferent to taking prisoners. They had no humanity. They had no compassion. Instead, they bound the captured ones' hands behind their backs, forced them down on their knees, and shot them in the backs of their heads, execution style. This barbaric act stripped the soldiers of all their pride and hope of ever surviving to see their loved ones again. This inhumane act minimized our soldiers to insignificant hollow bodies. Pharis didn't have any reason to believe that his destiny would be any different than that of his fellow soldiers who had already been shot. He had no reason to believe that he would be more fortunate than them. He had no reason to believe that his life would be spared. He expected to be shot just like the ones before him. He knew that the people back home, especially his mother, had been praying for his safety because he could feel it. While he appreciated their prayers, it seemed that his execution on July 20, 1950 was a done deal.

The North Koreans lined up the newly captured soldiers and aimed their machine guns at them. It reminded Pharis of the firing squads that he had seen in western movies. As they set their sights on Pharis, he thought of the family that he had left behind. Pharis remembered the fun that he and his sister Toot, now 15 years old, had before he left home. She was always throwing something at him to get his attention, whether it was dried cow paddies or hard cotton bolls, which always led to his chasing her down to punish her.

He remembered Bill, his 13 year old brother, and all the times they got into trouble together, like the time they tried to teach some puppies to swim, in a frozen lake. They weren't going to make the puppies swim alone. They had planned to go into the water too so they had stripped off all their clothes. When Mama found them and saw what they were up to, she broke off a switch from a nearby bush. As she marched them back home, still naked, she struck their bare cold legs with each step they took.

It was the two youngest siblings, Butch and Helen, just seven and four now, who concerned Pharis the most. They were so young when he left that they might not remember him when they got older.

The face of his hard-working, gentle, loving father for whom he had a great deal of respect and admiration came into Pharis' view. Dad would be crushed; he would feel responsible for Pharis' demise. What a guilt trip to lay on anyone!

Last but certainly not least, he saw the face of his sweet, loving mother, and knew that this would probably destroy her. She loved all her children but Pharis was her first born child; she had loved him longer. She might not ever recover from this. She had begged him not to join the Army. Why hadn't he listened to her? As he thought his life was about to end, he talked to his mother. He said, "Well Mama, what are you going to think about this?"

———✗✗✗———

My first memory of my childhood dates back to late August, 1949, a few months after my third birthday. Shortly after lunch, my mother was rocking me to coax me into taking an afternoon nap. Just before I dozed off, my mother said, "Look who is here!" I turned to check out the source of her excitement and saw the broad smile of my seventeen-year-old brother Pharis. He had come home from Ft. Jackson, Columbia, SC after completing thirteen weeks of basic training in the Army. What a great surprise! Pharis had never stayed away from home before. We all had missed him so much that the family just wasn't complete without him. I wriggled out of mother's arms and reached for Pharis' neck. At almost the same time, my mother sprang from the rocker and grabbed him on the other side. Then the back door flew open and all the others in the family came rushing in to participate in the homecoming. They had seen him coming into the house and rushed in to get their share of hugs and kisses too. We surrounded Pharis with everyone jockeying for their own space to get close to him, sometimes bumping someone else out of the way. Joy and excitement filled the room with everyone laughing and talking at the same time. The Greene family was complete again.

When the emotions finally subsided, Pharis announced that he had gifts for everyone. Wow! Not only had my big brother returned home but he had brought presents too. It seemed like Christmas in August! Pharis knelt down in front of me first and presented me with a little gold box with burgundy velvet on the outside. The inside contained a small gold bracelet with a heart on it, a treasure that I would cherish all my life. With all the excitement and presents to open, everyone forgot about my nap. No one expected me to miss this reunion.

There were five children born to Harlan and Maebelle Greene. Pharis is the oldest and I am the youngest. Dad was twenty-one and Mama was only fifteen when they married but they had a passionate love for each other that could only come straight from God. They were soul mates. Many years ago, I asked Mama how she and Daddy met. She said they met at a party and when she first saw him, she knew immediately that she wanted him to be her husband one day. Although he had already proposed to another woman, Mama got what she wanted. They married in Gaffney, SC on December 16, 1928.

Harlan, age 21, & Maebelle, age 15

We lived in the country in Rutherford County, NC where Dad worked as a sharecropper growing corn and cotton on the forty acres he had leased. Mama stayed at home to take care of the family's needs, cooking, sewing, and canning fruits and vegetables. If she had any spare time, she helped in the fields too. As soon as the children grew big enough, they all helped with the crops too. Being the youngest, I escaped most of the work in the fields.

Daddy loved farming. He enjoyed cultivating the earth, planting the seeds, and seeing the results of his labor. Farming, however, was really a difficult way to provide even the basic necessities for such a large family, especially when so many outside factors could determine the outcome of the crops. We had little control over some of the factors and no control over the largest one, the weather. If the weather didn't cooperate, the crops suffered, bringing in less money at the market. Money to feed and cloth five children was always scarce but we never thought of ourselves as being poor. In fact, we thought we were rich because we always had an unlimited amount of love and affection for each other and these didn't cost anything. Our parents instilled in us a strong sense of family pride and spiritual values. Both parents possessed a great sense of humor and playfulness which they passed on to all of us. Those qualities proved to be really important, especially when it seemed there was never enough money to take care of our family.

Chapter 1

—∽—

Before the Korean War

When Franklin Delano Roosevelt became the President of the United States in 1933, he had to face one of the nation's most extreme crises, the Great Depression which began on October 29, 1929. In his later years as President, he had to face another crisis, the worst war of all time, World War II.

Within hours after Roosevelt's inauguration on March 4, 1933, he moved decisively to get the country on the road to recovery. First he declared a "bank holiday" to stop the panic run on the nation's banks to withdraw money. He called a special session of Congress and ninety-nine days later, it passed some of the most significant laws and reforms in the nation's history. Roosevelt cut back on the federal payroll and veterans' pensions and reformed the nation's currency, finances, and banks. He provided funds for relief for the desperately poor, jobs on public work projects, and new terms for farmers, industries, and home mortgage holders.

With the help of Congress, Roosevelt established several institutions which are still in force today. The Tennessee Valley Authority (TVA) which involved building numerous dams that would produce cheap electricity. He established the National Labor Relations Act, giving

1

workers and the labor movement greater rights. He set up the Securities and Exchange Commission to regulate the stock market and protect investors. He established Social Security to provide pensions for the elderly.

Although Roosevelt had always enjoyed the life of an aristocrat, very soon after becoming President, he became known as the true friend of the common man. The American people loved his policies and they loved Roosevelt. His popularity became so great with the American people that, when he ran for his second term in 1936, he carried forty-six out of forty-eight states.

When World War II started in Europe in September, 1939, most Americans had little desire to get involved. In spite of the attitude of America, Roosevelt managed to provide support to the British but he had to be careful about America's involvement or he would risk losing his popularity. He traded ships to the British in exchange for bases. He provided them with easy loans and allowed American ships to fire on German ships to protect British convoys. Roosevelt felt that America was only involved from a distance.

In 1940, Roosevelt ran for the office of the President for an unprecedented third term, which inspired the 22nd Amendment limiting a president to two terms. His strict anti-war platform of "no Army abroad unless US is attacked" on her homeland helped him get re-elected. On December 7, 1941, when the Japanese aggressively bombed Pearl Harbor, Hawaii, an established territory of the US since June 14, 1900, Roosevelt was prepared to lead the United States into a full-scale war.

With the war lingering on in 1944, Roosevelt decided to run for another unprecedented fourth term convincing the American people that it would be unwise to change the Commander in Chief during a war. The Democratic Party, however, couldn't agree on who his running mate should be and proposed Harry S. Truman as a sort of an innocuous compromise between the split sides of the party. Both sides conceded and named Truman as the Vice-President candidate for the Democratic Party.

Unlike Roosevelt, Truman did not grow up in a privileged environment nor did he receive a formal education. He was the son of a farmer and West Point turned his application down due to his poor eyesight. Truman did not pursue acceptance to other colleges but instead worked at a variety of small jobs until taking over management of the family farm at age twenty-two. Truman's great love for reading enabled him to become a self-educated man.

As a young man, Truman joined the Missouri National Guard and entered World War I as a Lieutenant. He commanded an artillery battery in France and, after participating in several campaigns, returned home as a Captain. At age 35, Truman married his high school sweetheart, Bess Wallace, and opened a men's clothing store. His marriage was successful; his business was not. It failed after only three years.

Before becoming the Vice President candidate, Truman served ten years in the Senate but he possessed only minor political influence in the Democratic Party. No one, including Truman himself, believed that he was a man meant for high destiny.

Roosevelt and Truman won the election and Roosevelt started his 13ᵗʰ year as President of the US. On April 12, 1945, just 83 days after Roosevelt and Truman took their respective positions in the White House, Roosevelt died from a massive cerebral hemorrhage and Truman had to step into the shoes of the President. Until that time, not one in a million Americans could have imagined that Harry S. Truman would ever be President of the United States, let alone a good President.

Although many Americans were uncomfortable with that "little man" in the White House, Truman proceeded decisively from the beginning, presiding over the events of World War II and dealing with other Allied leaders. The war lingered on, over six years in Europe and almost four years since the bombing of Pearl Harbor. There had already been numerous casualties and Truman estimated that another million lives would be lost if the US and our allies had to invade Japan. Truman thought that these additional casualties would be a waste of human lives and decided the war needed to end. He made the toughest decision that any president before him had been forced to make. He decided to use the atomic bomb on Japan to end the war. On August 6, 1945, the US dropped the first bomb on Hiroshima; on August 9, 1945, we dropped the second bomb on Nagasaki. Truman ended the war saving a million lives but he was criticized harshly in later years for his decision. The world soon realized that this little man was capable of making very big decisions.

Truman continued Roosevelt's programs and implemented some of his own as he continued to fight communism. In spite of his good leadership, many felt that he had no chance of winning a re-election in 1948. The liberal Democrats nominated a Progressive party candidate and the Southern Democrats nominated their own Dixiecrat candidate, splitting the Democratic Party three ways. Truman himself didn't believe he had a chance to win nor did a Chicago newspaper which jumped the gun and printed its incautious banner headline for the next morning's paper which read, "Dewey Defeats Truman." To everyone's surprise, the Chicago newspaper got it wrong and Truman took over his second term as President, a term which would be dominated by the Korean War.

Chapter 2

—∽—

How the Korean War Started

M ost Americans and even some of the military personnel who served in Korea do not understand why and how the conflict started in Korea in 1950 between the North and the South. In fact, most Americans aren't familiar with the Korean War at all.

Going back over decades, several countries fought over the control of Korea but in 1910, Japan annexed Korea and took complete control of the country. Japan set up its government in Seoul, filled with generals who had been appointed by the Japanese emperor. The Korean people, deprived of freedom of assembly, association, the press, and speech, were forced to speak Japanese instead of their own native Korean language. Any rights that they may have enjoyed in the past had been taken away. When World War II ended in 1945 and we and our allies defeated the Japanese, Japan lost control of Korea.

Even though World War II started in Europe in 1939 and America got involved in 1941, the Soviet Union didn't join the United Nations' forces against Japan until August 8, 1945, two days after the US dropped the first atomic bomb on Japan. Before participating in the war, Joseph Stalin, the Soviet leader, asked US President Truman about allowing them to invade Korea which Truman had vowed would one day have its independence. Truman vetoed Stalin's suggestion stating that such an expedition would not be practical until after a successful landing had taken place on the Japanese mainland. Stalin subscribed to also support the independence of Korea; however, on the very next day, the Soviets went into action in Manchuria and landed on the northern half of Korea at the 38th parallel.

On August 11, 1945, just three days after the Soviets joined the war, Japan surrendered and the terms of their surrender were laid out. The terms stated that the Japanese forces above the 38th parallel would surrender to the Soviet Union; the Japanese forces below the 38th parallel would surrender to the US commander. A month after the entry of the Soviets into the war, on September 8th, American troops arrived in South Korea. Korea became two separate countries. The Soviets sealed off the 38th parallel claiming North Korea as its own. South Korea would be occupied by the US.

Recognizing the possibility of a confrontation with the Soviet Union, Truman acknowledged that the North Korea zone now belonged to the Soviets. The speculations as to the reasons the Soviets were awarded the upper half of Korea are many and probably all are true. The expedience in receiving the Japanese surrender, to prevent any single power's domination of Korea, and to stop the Soviet's advance south of the 38th parallel where it could take over Japan are some of the speculations. Not too bad a month for the Soviets. Enter a war at the very end after the enemy has been defeated, flex your muscles a little, and get awarded the upper part of Korea for an extremely small amount of effort.

Right away, both North and South Korea began to organize their respective police/military forces. As both sides strengthened, the occupants of both countries withdrew. The Soviet occupation forces withdrew from North Korea in December 1948, leaving behind 150 advisors for each army division for training purposes. The US occupation forces withdrew from South Korea on June 29, 1949, leaving behind about 500 men as a Korean Military Advisory Group (KMAG) to train the new armed forces.

By June 1950, the North Korean forces totaled 135,000 men including a tank brigade. China transferred another 12,000 North Korean soldiers back home who had been training and fighting in China. As early as 1949, the North Korean military had been sent to the Soviet Union for specialized training proving them to be far superior on battle expertise to the South Korean army. South Korea had a 98,000 man force, equipped with only small arms which were barely enough to deal with internal revolt and border attacks, let alone resist the North Korean army when it came South.

It is believed that both the Korean countries received monetary aid from both of their occupying countries. On October 6, 1949, the US granted South Korea $10.2 million for military aid and $110 million for economic aid for the year 1950, the first year of a three-year program. On March 15, 1950, the US Congress approved another $10.9 million for military aid for a total of $21.1 million. It is unsure the amount of money the Soviets granted to North Korea.

On March 17, 1949, the Soviets agreed to provide North Korea with heavy military equipment. Although the US had promised South Korea over $21 million for military aid, when the war broke out the military equipment was still en route leaving the South Korean forces totally unprepared to resist the invasion by the North Korean forces.

The planning of the invasion of South Korea by North Korea started at the end of World War II in 1945; at least it did in the mind of Kim Il Sung, the North Korean leader who had been appointed by the Soviet Union leader, Joseph Stalin. Kim had returned to North

Korea from fighting in China in the uniform of a Major of the Red Army and introduced as a national hero on October 14, 1945.

Kim had constantly begged Stalin to give him permission to invade South Korea, citing that he could reunite the South with the North as it had been before World War II ended. He boasted that the invasion would take only three weeks because, he claimed, the South was eager to reunite with the North. Kim had enviously watched Mao Zedong, the leader in China, reunite China after his final victory in their civil war in October, 1949 and wanted desperately to show Stalin that he was a much more capable leader and warrior than Mao. Stalin denied Kim's requests for over four years stating that there was no rush for an open conflict with the Americans in Korea. Kim really believed his own propaganda that if the Soviets would just get out of his way, he could conquer the Southern region in no time. He just needed a chance to prove it.

Meanwhile in South Korea, an American-educated, American-supported native and President of South Korea named Syngman Rhee had similar thoughts and beliefs. He believed that if only the Americans would remove their ridiculous restraints on him and get out of his way, he could conquer North Korea in no time. As a young man, Rhee had taken a stand against the Japanese back in 1919, had become a political prisoner, and had barely missed being executed. He had been forced to take refuge in the US where he received a Harvard degree and a Ph.D. from Princeton. Now a man in his 70's, he thought that he still possessed the fortitude to reunite the North and the South and destroy the North Korean's communist government.

Stalin began to reconsider granting Kim's numerous requests to invade South Korea when he heard about the speech given by US Secretary of State Dean Acheson on January 12, 1950 at the National

Press Club in Washington. Acheson's speech seemed to send a signal that America's Asian defense perimeter did not include Korea and Stalin got the distinct feeling that the Americans might stay out of any conflict in Korea. Acheson had been trying to explain the American policy in Asia after China had fallen to the Communists. Instead he sent an extremely dangerous message to the Communist world: America would not get involved if South Korea's enemies threatened them. Again on May 2, 1950, America sent a similar message to the Communists. In an interview with "US News and World Report", Chairman of the Senate Foreign Relations Committee, Senator Tom Connally of Texas, stated that the Republic of Korea would be abandoned in case of enemy aggression and the security of the nation was *not* essential to America's defensive Asian strategy.

After these two comments from the Americans and numerous confirmations from Kim and China's Mao that America would not get involved with any conflict in Korea, Stalin finally gave his permission for Kim to invade South Korea but with the understanding that he must follow specific guidelines. Under no circumstances, Stalin stated, would he have his fingerprints on this invasion nor would he come to Kim's rescue should he get into trouble. Stalin also required Kim to seek Mao's advice and cooperation and even his troops for backup if necessary. Kim agreed to follow Stalin's guidelines. They named the invasion "In Min Gun".

Kim met with Mao, a more seasoned and wiser leader, who agreed to assist Kim in his ambitious venture. Mao thought that Kim would have appreciated the opportunity to learn from Mao's experience and success but instead, Mao found Kim to be arrogant. His audacity, what the Chinese saw as his brashness, surprised the Chinese leader. Who did Kim think he was? Unfortunately, Mao had just seen the first glimpse of Kim's contemptuous attitude and Mao would soon realize that Kim had his own agenda. He had his own plans for this invasion, no matter what Mao advised him to do. Now that Stalin had given Kim the green light to invade South Korea, Kim was determined to do it his way, as long as Stalin wasn't watching.

Chapter 3

—መ—

Pharis

Pharis Lynell Greene was born on May 17, 1932 in Bostic, NC, the first-born child to Harlan and Maebelle, now twenty-five and nineteen years old. He also enjoyed the status of the first-born grandchild on both sides of the family and needless to say, he was showered with love and attention giving him a strong sense of confidence and independence. He loved being the only child until almost three years later when his baby sister Margaret joined the family. Then two years later, his brother Bill came along.

Without much entertainment on the farm, the three of them had to find ways to amuse themselves. They had to invent their own fun-filled activities. While their creativity was to be commended, it often resulted in their getting into some kind of trouble with our parents on a daily basis. Both parents wanted to make sure that they raised their children right, so most days they got a "switching" when they misbehaved. Pharis said that if Mama missed a day switching him, he asked her if he had done something to make her mad at him. He asked her if she didn't love him anymore.

*Maebelle and Harlan
holding Pharis*

*Left to right –Bill,
Pharis age 7,
and Margaret*

*Pharis, age 12,
Margaret and Bill*

The three children formed such a sibling bond that they were almost inseparable. Their group was the perfect size and they liked being the only three. Then almost seven years later, another brother C.B. joined them. The three older ones had built such a close relationship among themselves that it might not have room for another child, especially one whose size wouldn't allow him to keep up with their daily shenanigans. Since C.B. had already arrived, they realized that they would have to adapt to having him around, but Pharis vowed he would have a talk with Mama about bringing any more children into the family. He told her that if another baby came along, he would leave home. Ouch!! In spite of his threats, two and a half years later I became the fifth child. For a long time I wondered if I had been the reason Pharis joined the Army. Mama said she knew that he didn't mean what he said about leaving home. She said that Pharis, now thirteen years old, couldn't keep his hands off me. She said that any time he disappeared, she always found him standing at my crib entertaining me with his funny faces and baby talk.

Front–C.B.
L to R, Margaret, Helen, Grandma Dobbins, Pharis, Bill,
and cousin Bobby

At age sixteen, Pharis felt a great sense of duty to serve his country and fight for its freedom. He wanted to join the Army but needed our parents' consent but they refused. He was just too young they said. His determination to enlist in the Army left him compelled to take matters into his own hands. He forged our parents' signatures on the military forms but fortunately the recruiter caught it. Pharis' persistency continued until shortly after his seventeenth birthday, his tenacity paid off. He finally convinced our parents to sign the paperwork giving their permission for him to join, a decision that both parents would soon regret.

Helen and C. B.   *Pharis, age 17, at Ft. Jackson, SC*

Pharis officially joined the Army on May 24, 1949. No one felt that Pharis had deserted the family when every hand was needed on the farm because later he helped financially by sending home sometimes as much as $50 each month, a huge amount in those days.

After a short visit home from basic training, Pharis reported to Ft. Eustis in Virginia where he received training in ship-to-shore landings. He finished several weeks of this special training and came home again before leaving to go overseas. When the orders came for him to report to duty, Daddy took him to Charlotte, NC where he boarded a train headed for Camp Stoneman, CA, stopping in Atlanta, Dallas, Los Angeles, and finally San Francisco. On the train, he and a few other soldiers met a nice older lady who befriended them. Pharis said she appeared to have plenty of money because she generously bought them cocktails all the way to California making the long ride much more enjoyable.

Pharis was first assigned to Company "I" of the 31st Regiment which was a part of the 7th Infantry Division. This unit had won wide acclaim for their gallant deeds during WWII and during the thirty-three years of continuous overseas service that it had given its country. The unit had never been stationed within the continental limits of the US. It was one of the units subjected to the infamous Bataan Death March in 1942, a march on the Island of Luzon in the Philippines when the Japanese military held them captive.

At the port in California, Pharis boarded a ship headed for Japan. On December 24, 1949, he arrived in Yokohama located on the eastern side of the main island near Tokyo. Previously Pharis had barely left the farm and he had certainly never traveled abroad. Now he found himself halfway around the world in a foreign country where most of the natives didn't speak English, in snow and cold temperatures like he had never experienced before. He wondered to himself, "What have I gotten myself into?"

At home on the farm, Pharis had always felt safe and protected, not the same as he felt when he arrived in Japan. The joke in our family was that Mama had been so protective of him that she had never allowed him to eat with a fork for fear he would hurt himself. He claims that wasn't true. He claims that it was just too hard to round up those little green peas that he loved so much with a fork. While this new adventure excited him, at the same time he felt unsettled and a little scared. Already he missed his friends and his family, especially his mother.

As soon as he got settled, he eagerly wrote his family to tell them about his new life. In his first letter dated December 31, 1949, he told them that after his arrival in Japan on Christmas Eve, he boarded a train and rode all night until he arrived at a replacement company just outside of Sendai, north of Tokyo, on Christmas morning. He had eaten a big Christmas dinner and remained there for three days while he recuperated from the trip and adjusted to the environment.

Pharis then traveled to the northern part of the big island, took a ferry across the canal, and arrived at Camp Crawford on the island called Hokkaido, located on the northern part of Japan just 300 miles from the Soviet Union. Even though it was cold with about three feet of snow on the ground and more snow expected, he thought he'd like it there. He wrote, "There are some pretty good guys in the company."

Pharis's first letter contained the usual small talk about everyone in the family and about the girls he left behind in the States. He asked if Ruth got married and talked about the beautiful girls in Japan. He passed advice on to all. He wrote to tell Toot (Margaret) not to marry Bowman until he got back home. Tell Dad to watch her. Tell Bill to be a good little boy and stay away from the girls. Tell the kids (C. B. and Helen) hello. And to Dad he wrote, "How did you make out on that tractor payment?" He signed, "Love Lucky". The letter contained the normal chatter of a seventeen-year-old boy.

In the following few months Pharis wrote many similar letters addressing his mother as "My Little Girl" and "My Favorite Girl" and to his sister Toot as "Darling". In most of the letters, he gave advice to his younger siblings. He advised Toot to keep playing basketball and one day she might be good and not to drop out of school. He advised Bill to stay in school at all costs. He continuously asked for pictures of the family especially ones of Butch (C.B.) and Helen. Pharis worried about the health of his Grandpa and Grandma Dobbins and continually sent his wishes for their quick recoveries. He expressed his concerns about the family's poor crops and wished that he could be home to help.

Grandpa & Grandma Dobbins

All of the letters normally addressed the weather, now fifteen to twenty degrees below zero, which he seemed to be getting accustomed to. He talked about the snow, now about five to six feet deep. Pharis wrote about his field trips, lasting from one to several days, on which they marched thirty to forty miles away from the base in wet, freezing weather. When they arrived at their destination, they dug through several feet of snow to set up a camp underneath. Then they actually slept under the mounds of snow. These field trips left them extremely exhausted but mostly they slept warm. When they arose in the mornings, they felt like they were freezing for awhile but soon adjusted to the cold. "It wasn't so bad," he wrote.

Some days in a blizzard, they had to hike several miles in snow shoes. Pharis and three other guys had the responsibility of leading and breaking the trail for the others. This left all of them, especially the ones out front, physically drained but they still had to go out again the next day.

Pharis wrote about his military duties and assignments. He was first assigned to the heavy weapons platoon, then applied for the position of clerk typist, but remained in the field because his superior officer told him, "Lt. Morgan needs a gunner for the 57." Pharis was referring to a 57 Recoilless Rifle which looks similar to a bazooka or rocket launcher. He applied for the position of a cook but again his superior officer told him that they needed him more in the field as a mortar operator.

The military, at least where Pharis was stationed, enforced their strict rules. Pharis reported, "You have to walk a straight line or spend time in the stockades." One kid broke into the supply room and received a five-year sentence. If you missed the bed check at 11:00 PM, you received seven days of hard labor as your punishment. On one occasion, Pharis and a few of his buddies went into town to see their girlfriends. All of them were having too much fun and didn't want to leave so they stayed, for two days, knowing what the punishment would be. He didn't worry about the hard labor because as he said, "I have done it before and I can pull it again." In addition to the hard labor, Pharis' reprimand included a reduction in his paycheck of eight dollars each month. Obviously they thought those trips into town for a few days had been worth the consequences.

In his letters Pharis continued to inquire about the girls he had left behind and wrote about the beautiful women he had met in Japan and about his social life. In his letter dated April 13, 1950, he said that he had gone to a movie, the first night in three weeks that he had not gone into town. He had broken up with his Japanese girlfriend and asked that we keep the girls back home single until he returned. He signed, "Your Prodigal Son".

Pharis was adjusting to his military life. "This wasn't so bad," he wrote. He might consider re-enlisting in the Army for another six years after his contract for the initial three years expired. He wrote that if he decided to re-enlist, he didn't want any girls back home trying to change his mind. While he didn't want to get serious with any one girl, he continued to send messages to some of them through his family, like Dorothy. "Tell her I still love her, as much as I ever did," he joked.

```
                    "Dream Boy"

          If you've ever met a nice boy
             I'm sure you will agree
          That mine is just as nice
             As any boy could be.

          He's just an average soldier boy
             with the mind of any lad
          Many times I've seen him laugh
             And he's almost never sad.

          He is tall and handsome
             like the boy in most girls dreams
          Too, he's just as cute as cute can be
             so he's strictly on the beam.

          If you've ever seen him
             I'm sure you'll say the same
          And if you haven't guessed it
             PHARIS GREENE is his name.

                    EDITH
```

If Pharis' family didn't already worry about him, without knowing it Pharis gave them more reasons to worry. He wrote about attending his first military funeral. One of his fellow soldiers had shot himself because, everyone surmised, he feared he might be court-martialed. Pharis said that this was one of the three suicides that had occurred in the last three months. He wrote that no one back home should worry about him doing anything like that because he was having a "wonderful time". "Tell everyone hello," signed "Lucky".

Our family belonged to a Southern Baptist church and had very strong spiritual values. He wrote his family requesting that everyone back home pray for him; he was certainly doing a lot of praying himself.

When Dad shared with Pharis a vision that he had in which the Lord spoke to him, Pharis said that he understood because the Lord had spoken to him too.

Pharis at Camp Crawford in Japan

On June 29, 1950, Pharis wrote what was to be his last letter home for a long time. It started with **"Hello Mom, how is My Little Girl getting along tonight? I hope you feel better than I do."** Pharis expressed concerns about Dad's crops not doing well and about Grandpa's poor health. Then he wrote, **"I guess you've heard the latest about Korea. It doesn't sound too good, especially to us. I just hope they get it stopped before the 24th (Division) has to go down there. It would be bad if they sent us because we would spoil all their fun by ending it too soon."**

He completed the letter on a lighter note. He had just returned from a movie starring Buster Crabb, one that he thought Bill would like. He reminded Toot not to get married. He inquired if Butch liked school and that Helen hadn't started school yet, had she? Pharis asked how Dad was getting along with his tractor and did he need a nice calm driver who would be easy on it, one who would never speed. He went on to talk about an oil painting of Toot that he planned to send home and about getting his false teeth put in to replace the four front ones that had been pulled earlier.

Pharis didn't always tell the family everything that happened. For instance, he didn't tell them about the thirteen teeth that he had filled, without the luxury of anesthesia, by an Oriental female dentist. The incident no doubt helped prepare Pharis for the pain that he would have to endure from the brutal beatings and torture that he was about to experience in Korea. He signed his letter, "Your Prodigal Son, Pharis", the last words that his family would read from him for a long time.

In just a few short months, the words of a seventeen-year-old boy had become more mature, more like the words of a grown man. All of Pharis' letters showed what kind of man he had become. He had become a man who shared a close relationship with his family and who loved and respected every one of them. He had become a man who felt concern about his family's well-being and compassion for their problems. He had become a man with a huge heart, a man not afraid to express his love and affection. His letters showed that he had become a man who loved his country and was willing to pay any price, even the ultimate price, to defend her against any enemy's aggression. He was a son, a grandson, a brother. He was a true and faithful American; he was an American soldier.

Chapter 4

—⁓—

Unprepared for War

In 1950 when the North Koreans invaded South Korean, Truman called it a "police action". America had finished the war in the Pacific just five years earlier and he did not want the American people to panic thinking they were in another war. WWII had left the US strapped financially and its military forces and weapons in shambles. Many of the seasoned military men, after having fought courageously and ferociously for several years, had gone home to their families to stay. Our military forces were left with inadequate numbers and inexperienced personnel, but the lack of qualified officers was the worst of its dilemma.

President Truman wanted to keep taxes down and, at the same time, pay off its debts from the last war. Congress cut the defense budget to its lowest possible level. No money remained in the budget for military training or weapons and none would be allocated for the country's defense.

According to author David Halberstam, in addition to the lack of experienced troops and sufficient weapons, the US had other problems when the Korean War began. In his book, *The Coldest Winter,* he claimed that the American military stationed in Japan had everything on their minds *except* the possibility of combat with any enemy. Halberstam's book claimed that no training for combat had been taking place and no one had been trying to get the troops accustomed to the rough mountainous terrain and the treacherous below zero temperatures, both conditions almost identical to those found in Korea. He wrote that even the lowest ranked soldiers were undisciplined and disrespectful of the military and its officers and that they had grown soft and spoiled with the good life in Japan. The military became preoccupied with having a "shack girl" or a "house boy" who took care of their every need allowing the soldiers to become complacent and lazy. Critics claimed that some Americans felt superior to the Asians, especially after being triumphant in World War II, and underestimated the capabilities of the North Koreans. Halberstam stated that Keyes Beech, a Marine veteran of WWII, wrote in the "Chicago Daily News" that the first American soldiers sent to Korea were "spiritually, mentally, morally, and physically unprepared for war".

Maybe that was true for some of the soldiers who were stationed in Japan but that certainly was not the situation in the 31st Infantry and it certainly wasn't true for PFC Pharis Greene. The training in his unit included rigorous physical activities and days and weeks of maneuvers in the snow in subzero weather. Pharis spent many hours training on the rocket launcher or bazooka, machine guns, and the M-1 Rifle. Some of the authors who wrote about the Korean War correctly stated that the weapons that our military was forced to use were inadequate and out-of-date. Most of the weapons had been left over from World War II but these old, insufficient weapons were all that our troops had to work with.

From the time Pharis arrived in northern Japan in December, 1949 through the month of March, it snowed almost daily. Each time a new snow storm arrived, the 31st Regiment packed up their gear and marched thirty to forty miles from their warm and sheltered camp. When they arrived at their destination, they had to dig down several feet to set up camp under the mounds of snow. Pharis remembered many times digging so deep that the length of his arm and the shovel combined was barely sufficient to get the snow out to the top of the bunker where he would be spending many nights. Perhaps that acclamation to the cold weather that Pharis endured during training gave him the fortitude to survive the next three winters in Korea.

Since the partition of Korea into the North and the South in 1945, there had always been a certain level of simmering military tension between the two regions, especially at the border on the 38th parallel. It was nothing too large but enough to keep each side off balance, and then something started to change. There had been signs of a tension buildup in the weeks before the assault. The American intelligence reports were checked out daily but somehow these signs of trouble slipped through the cracks.

A young American intelligence agent, Jack Singlaub, who had formerly served in China with the Office of Strategic Services (OSS), now the CIA, grew more and more suspicious about the activities of the North Koreans. He sent a group of South Korean agents whom he had been training, north to look for indicators that the capitol of North Korea, Pyongyang, might be planning something covert. He instructed them to look for the simplest of things especially near the border. When they returned from their mission, they reported that North Korea had started restoring railroads and rebuilding bridges, strong enough to hold the heavy Soviet-supplied T-34 tanks. The homes near the border had been deserted, another sign that something big was getting ready to happen.

Singlaub wasn't likely to pass this information on to General Douglas MacArthur, a five-star general stationed in Tokyo, who was in command of the Far East military. Singlaub knew the information would stop there. MacArthur may have been a hero to most Americans after World War II but Singlaub had known him before and knew that MacArthur hated the OSS and the Eastern establishment types who had been so influential in the OSS and effectively controlled it. MacArthur had his own philosophy: control intelligence and you control decision-making. Singlaub had no confidence that MacArthur would pass the information on to the people who should be making the decisions about the unsettling changes taking place.

George Kennan, head of the US State Department's Policy Planning staff, was considered to be the leading expert in the US government on the subject of the Soviet Union and its intentions. There could be no doubt that he possessed a superb knowledge of the Soviet Union, China, their histories and their politics. After returning from one of his trips to Tokyo, he expressed his deep suspicions of the quality and competence of MacArthur's staff, especially his intelligence people. They didn't seem to be on top of the new and possibly dangerous activities surrounding them.

Then in May and June, 1950, some of Kennan's people at the State Department's Policy Planning group began picking up sounds that something big was about to happen and they placed the entire Communist world under intense scrutiny. They decided it wasn't the Soviet Union or any of their Eastern European satellites. Perhaps it could be Korea but that was quickly ruled out by the American military. The South Korean forces were too well armed and trained, clearly superior to the North Koreans. The North Koreans wanted no conflict with the South Koreans on the battlefield. With this kind of reassurance from the military, the government believed that the threat couldn't be coming from North Korea. After all, the American military wouldn't intentionally mislead the government, would it? Everyone was in denial about what was getting ready to happen. How could the US be prepared if everyone were in denial? If a problem isn't recognized, a solution is certainly not forthcoming.

Chapter 5

—ɯ—

The Invasion

In early summer of 1950, life in South Korea was good in an ancient kind of way. There were no cars or equipment for farming since the Japanese had taken everything from them when they were forced out of Korea, but they were doing all right. They had adjusted to not having the bare essentials and had learned to make do with what they had; they had no other choice. The children were going to school, even learning English, and playing kickball and soccer in the yards and fields. Life was peaceful in South Korea in the early summer of 1950. Korea had been called the "Land of the Morning Calm" but that all changed in a matter of minutes.

Suddenly at the crack of dawn on Sunday, June 25, 1950, everything in the lives of the South Korean people was turned upside down. Life as they knew it would never be the same. Unprovoked and unannounced, as many as 100,000 North Korean soldiers crossed the 38th parallel border and attacked South Korea. It was like D-Day in 1944; there was no warning. Everyone was in a state of shock and at least two and a half hours passed, from 4:00 AM until 6:30 AM, until Syngman Rhee, President of South Korea, received the news. The Americans still had not been alerted. At 8:45 AM, a United Press reporter, Jack James, talked to a Marine guard about the events taking place. The Marine tried to convince the correspondent that the North Koreans crossed the border all the time, that it was a common occurrence. James replied, "Yeah, but this time they've got tanks!" The invasion was totally unexpected and the South Koreans were completely caught off guard; they were totally unprepared.

At 9:50 AM. on Sunday in Korea (8:50 PM on Saturday in Washington), one of the military intelligent agents suggested to James that Washington should be notified. James agreed and sent an urgent wire to Washington that read,

> *"URGENT UNPRESS NEW YORK 25095 JAMES FRAGMENTARY REPORT EXTHIRTY EIGHT PARRALLEL INDICATED NORTH KOREANS LAUNCHED SUNDAY MORNING ATTACKS GENERALLY ALONG ENTIRE BORDER PARA REPORTS AT ZERO NINETHIRTY LOCAL TIME INDICATED KAESONG FORTY MILES NORTHWEST SEOUL AND HEADQUARTERS OF KOREAN ARMY'S FIRST DIVISION FELL NINE AM STOP ENEMY FORCES REPORTED THREE TO FOUR KILOMETERS SOUTH OF BORDER ON ONJIN PENINSULA STOP TANKS SUPPOSED BROUGHT INTO USE CHUNCHON FIFTY MILES NORTH WEST SEOUL...."*

James' wire, the first notice regarding the invasion of South Korea, reached Washington late Saturday evening when the American government was scattered but arrived in time to make the Sunday paper. President Harry S. Truman had stopped in Baltimore to dedicate a new airport, Baltimore Friendship, and had later flown home to Independence, Missouri. Secretary of State, Dean Acheson, had gone to his farm in Maryland. Some of Acheson's subordinates notified him of the North Korean invasion but he checked his sources carefully before alerting the President. Truman wanted desperately to return to Washington to work on the solution to this problem, but Acheson convinced him that any change in his normal schedule might send the wrong message to other countries.

On June 25, 1950, the latest war of communist conquest had begun. It could have been the beginning of World War III if the US had not acted immediately.

On June 26, Korean time, the United Nations Security Council approved a resolution describing the invasion of South Korea as a "breach of the peace and an action of aggression" and called upon the members to render all their assistance to South Korea as might be necessary to restore peace. Eventually sixteen member nations sent armed contingents to assist in the fighting.

On June 27, 1950, President Truman issued the order for US air and naval forces to resist Communist aggression in Korea. The US was the first of the United Nations to send in military forces. In an emotional speech by Senator Robert Taft on the Senate floor, Truman was criticized for not getting the approval of Congress before proceeding. At the same time, Taft asked for the resignation of Secretary of State Dean Acheson, stating that Acheson's policies on Asia were seriously flawed. That resignation didn't happen.

Chapter 6

—ɯ—

MacArthur and Truman

G eneral Douglas MacArthur was serving in Tokyo when he received the news of the attack by the North Koreans. Born in Little Rock, Arkansas, seventy-year-old MacArthur was the son of General Arthur MacArthur who served in the Civil War. Douglas MacArthur's military record was exemplary, starting with his days at West Point where he received the highest grades ever recorded there and obtained the rank of first captain, the highest honor in the cadet corps. At age fifty, President Hoover named him chief of staff with four stars, the highest military post in the US. MacArthur's military expertise, especially during WWII, made him a living legend. In 1942, MacArthur was awarded his fifth star as a general. Both MacArthur and his father were awarded the Congressional Medal of Honor, the only father and son in history to be so honored. In 1945, President Truman appointed MacArthur as Supreme Commander of the Allied Powers (SCAP).

When MacArthur heard about the invasion, he was surprisingly slow to react. His actions worried some of his people around him because he seemed extremely indifferent. When the invasion started, just by chance, John Foster Dulles and John Allison happened to be on a trip to Seoul and Tokyo. They both worked with the State Department and were connected to the US national security group.

They attended a briefing that first Sunday night, June 25, and reported that MacArthur seemed far too relaxed under the circumstances. MacArthur told Dulles and Allison that the first reports of the invasion were inconclusive and it was probably only a reconnaissance in force. MacArthur was quoted as saying, "If Washington only will not hobble me, I can handle it with one arm tied behind my back." MacArthur added that, by the way, Rhee had asked for some fighter planes but he didn't think the South Koreans knew how to use them. In any event, he said he intended to send a few just for morale support.

While Dulles and Allison were temporarily relieved, their fears were soon heightened when they spoke to others outside of MacArthur's court. Brigadier General Crump Garvin, commander of the Port of Yokohama, confided to them that there had been reports coming through the 8th Army Intelligence for the past two or three weeks. The reports stated that the civilians near the North Korean side of the parallel were being moved away and that the North Koreans were concentrating large numbers of troops just above the border. He continued, "Anyone who read the reports could see something was going to happen and soon." He said he didn't know what MacArthur and his crowd had been doing but they certainly had not been paying attention to the intelligence reports.

On Monday, June 26, Ambassador Muccio, the senior American State Department representative in Korea, ordered the immediate evacuation of American women and children from the country. MacArthur suggested to Muccio that the move was premature and insisted, "There is no reason to panic in Korea."

That night Dulles and Allison went separate ways for dinner. Allison's dinner party was constantly being interrupted by the comings and goings of journalists and diplomats, all of them checking with their sources, and returning with somber reports. Dulles had dinner with GEN MacArthur. Dulles later reported that there had been no news regarding the invasion. In fact, no one had interrupted their dinner and they had watched a movie, the General's favorite form of entertainment, after dinner.

Dulles and Allison were scheduled to fly back to the US the next day and were waiting at the Haneda Airport for a delayed plane. Unexpectedly, MacArthur joined them. Both were shocked by the change in MacArthur; he was a transformed man. MacArthur was no longer the confident, jaunty figure who had assured them only two days earlier that the action of the North Koreans was only a recon mission. MacArthur was now completely despondent. Dulles and Allison had heard rumors that MacArthur was known to suffer from mood swings, but they never expected him to display such a volatile personality. MacArthur said, "The only thing we can do is get our people safely out of the country." He was totally dejected, completely forlorn.

When a message came that the Secretary of the Army wanted a telecom meeting with the General at 1:00 PM, MacArthur ignored the message. It must have been extremely important for Washington to reach MacArthur to talk to its commander in the field to find out what he thought should be done in this major crisis. Surprisingly, MacArthur told his aides that he was too busy seeing Dulles and Allison off and Washington would have to talk to his chief of staff.

Over the first thirty-six hours after the invasion, news regarding Korea reached Washington in spurts. The most serious of the information received was a cable from Dulles and Allison. They said that if the South Koreans couldn't hold the North Koreans, the US should intervene. The cable read, "To sit by while South Korea is overrun by an unprovoked armed attack would start a disastrous chain of events leading most probably to world war."

Before the North Koreans invaded South Korea, GEN MacArthur's attention had been focused almost exclusively on political developments in Japan. He was trying to shape a defeated country into a more democratic society. It became very clear that MacArthur wanted no part of Korea in the period from 1945 to 1950. When General John Hodge, the American Commander in South Korea, pleaded for MacArthur's assistance or his advice, MacArthur told him to take care of Korea himself. MacArthur said, "I wouldn't put my foot in Korea. It belongs to the State Department." And, he didn't put his foot in Korea before 1950 but one time, and that was very briefly. After the invasion, MacArthur set foot in Korea only fourteen times but never spent the night.

It was no secret that President Truman and GEN MacArthur were not friends. In fact, they barely tolerated each other. MacArthur felt superior to Truman; he felt superior to all men, except Washington and Lincoln. Those two were the only ones he considered his peers. In his mind, MacArthur thought that he was already a great national hero in those hard pre-World War II years while Truman was still going from failure to failure in the early 1930's. MacArthur had been disrespectful of Truman from the start and did not try to hide his distaste for Truman, the Commander in Chief.

When Dulles returned from a meeting with MacArthur in Tokyo, he recommended a change of commanders. He said that MacArthur seemed too old and he was bothered by the way his attention span seemed to waver. President Truman and his senior military men believed that McArthur had begun behaving badly almost as soon as World War II ended. Truman had seriously considered relieving MacArthur of his duties on several occasions, but remembered how much the American people loved him. MacArthur had been built up to heroic stature and the decision to relieve him might hurt Truman politically with the American people.

Since the US was the first to respond to the invasion of South Korea and was supplying most of the men and money, the UN gave the US the responsibility of choosing a leader for all the countries involved. No matter how Truman felt about MacArthur, Commander of the US Army, he knew that we needed organized and unified leadership during this crisis. Other members of the UN had already starting sending in their military and certainly there was a great deal more to come. Truman also knew that his choice for this position had to have the experience and the ability to make tough decisions and the choices for this position were slim. Truman thought that it was too late to change horses now; he thought he was stuck with MacArthur.

Reluctantly, on July 10, 1950, President Truman officially appointed GEN Douglas MacArthur as Commander in Chief of the UN forces in this Korean "police action". Most Americans knew MacArthur as a fearless and capable warrior and GEN MacArthur was well respected and loved by the people of all countries in the free world. Most Americans who did not know MacArthur well thought that Truman had made an excellent choice but the President of the United States was not so sure. All he knew was that he was about to go to war in a distant land, his armed forces commanded by a general he not only disliked but, more importantly, distrusted but he feared replacing him would create far greater problems for him politically.

Truman would find his presidency severely damaged by his lack of ability to control MacArthur, but then no one controlled MacArthur. While GEN MacArthur would find his place in history, he would also be severely damaged by his failure to respect and to take the full measure of the President.

Chapter 7

—ɷ—

America Responds

On June 28, 1950, just three days after the North Koreans' invasion, Seoul, the capital of South Korea located about 60 miles from the border at the 38th parallel, had fallen to the North Korean Red Communists and most of the South Korean Army had been destroyed. On June 30, President Truman extended his original orders of sending in air and naval support and ordered the US ground troops in Japan to report to Korea immediately.

The American 21st, 34th, and 19th Regiments, all part of the 24th Division, were slated to be the first units to go to Korea. A Division usually consists of up to 15,000 soldiers, but in Korea it often consisted of only 12,000 soldiers. The 24th Division was short on men, especially officers, and other soldiers had to be re-assigned as "replacements" from other divisions. Pharis and about 275 other men were re-assigned to the 24th Division, all of whom were non-commissioned officers (NCO's) except Pharis who was an enlisted PFC. Pharis was placed with the 34th Regiment, Company "K".

The 24th Division was ordered to get to Korea as quickly as possible and move up the west side of South Korea, until it met up with the onrushing enemy, believed to be near the village of Suwon just south of Seoul.

MG William Dean, commander of the 24th Division, was a big man of six feet, fifty-five years old, with a bulldog face and an aggressive stance. Dean was known as a rigid military man who demanded absolute adherence to forms and rules. This was not his first assignment in Korea. He had become the military governor of South Korea in October, 1947 for about a year until the elections established a republic. With this new assignment in Korea, he made what military analysts believe to be a critical mistake. Instead of concentrating his limited forces in one position where they might be able to maximize their firepower, unwisely Dean decided to split up his units.

The first US group of troops to leave for South Korea was the 21st Regiment, called, "Task Force Smith", led by LTC Charles B. (Brad) Smith. Smith, now thirty-four years old, was a good-looking young man, medium height, with a strong and compact body. He had graduated from West Point in 1939 and held a competent record for his services in the Pacific in World War II.

Smith's troops were air-lifted in Air Force C-54 Skymasters from Japan to Pusan, a port located above the 35th parallel on the southeast coast of South Korea. It took two days for the 21st Regiment to arrive in South Korea due to the shortage of planes and the extremely foggy weather in which the planes couldn't fly. Pharis remembered hearing that one plane attempted to fly in the heavy fog but unfortunately crashed, killing about 20 American soldiers.

Smith had been ordered to get to Korea as soon as possible; time was of the essence. Smith waited for most of the 21st soldiers to arrive at the Pusan port but decided he couldn't afford to wait any longer. He had to get to his destination and delay the North Koreans from advancing south until more of our forces could get to Korea. The ones with the 21st who had arrived were transported by train to Taejon, located closer to the west side of South Korea above the 36th parallel. They arrived on the morning of July 3, 1950.

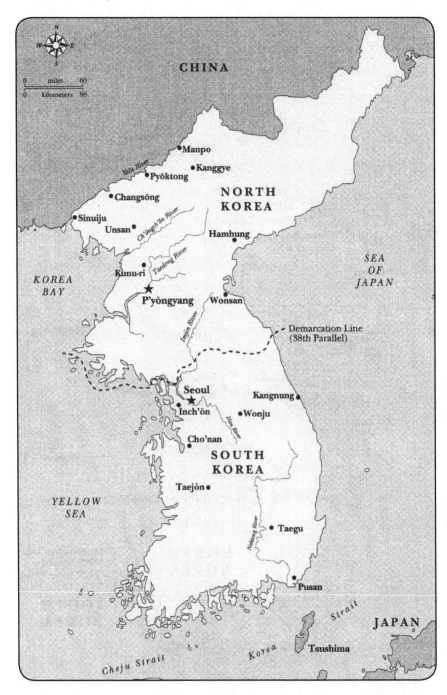

When the US troops arrived in Korea, you could recognize them from their broad smiles and the spring in their strides. They weren't scared; they were cocky; they were American soldiers. But these American soldiers had no idea what was in store for them. Only ten percent of the soldiers arriving were veterans; the rest were very young men, some teenagers, with no battle experience. Their fighting ability, however, would be put to the most extreme tests. From the very first day, if these young men were to survive, they would need to be converted into veterans overnight.

At Taejon, LTC Brad Smith met with Brigadier General John Church, an elderly officer not known for his vitality. Church had, however, been put in charge of the survey team sent to Korea by MacArthur to find out what was needed and where.

Church had moved his headquarters back from Suwon to Taejon, some 90 miles, because the North Korean army, called the "In Min Gun", had been bearing down on him. Still, in all his cockiness, Church told Smith that all he needed was a few GI's who would not fear a few tanks to stand up to the enemy. Church then pointed at a map and told Smith to take a stand near Osan, just south of Suwon.

On July 4th, Smith took about 540 men, an under-strength battalion (which normally consisted of 700-850 soldiers), boarded a train and headed north toward Ansong. At the Ansong station, the South Koreans cheered the US troops which made them feel proud, because it showed that they were the good guys, the heroes who had come to rescue a scared people. Looking back, the South Koreans may have been happy that our troops had arrived, but it was more likely that they were happy the train had arrived in order for them to flee south. Either way, their welcome by the locals made our troops feel good about themselves and their mission if only for a short while.

The spirit of the American troops was high. They were convinced that their stay in Korea would be at worst just a few days. They weren't even sure why they were there; they were told that this was just a "police action", no big deal. They believed that, once the North Koreans saw the American uniforms, they would turn and run. They were told that the North Korean soldiers were poorly trained and less than half of them had weapons of any kind. They should be back in Japan in no time so most of them brought only two days of C-rations.

Because of this misconception, they were also not prepared for battle. The weaponry taken with them was scarce. Each soldier carried either an M-1 rifle or a carbine, with less than 100 rounds of ammunition. A company, with only 140 men, two-thirds the number for wartime missions, carried three light machine guns, with four boxes of ammunition per gun. There was only one Browning automatic rifle with 200 rounds for each platoon. The weapons platoon had only three 60mm mortars and 75mm recoilless rifles, but they had not taken sufficient ammunition for the rifles. No one brought any hand grenades. There was no reason to be concerned that they were ill prepared; after all, this was just a simple police action.

No one told our soldiers that our handful of men would be fighting an army. No one told them that our small group of military had to beat back five communist divisions. No one told them that the battle would be between our guts and their tanks. Maybe it was a good thing that no one told them. They only knew that their mission was called Operation Delay and their purpose was to delay the North Korean army until reinforcements from the US and the UN arrived. At no time did they understand that police action involved any type of combat.

As they passed some of the South Korean soldiers who were coming back from the front line, there was an urge to ask them what it was like closer to the battlefield, but the South Korean soldiers didn't have to speak to tell their stories. Their boots, their clothes, their faces, and their eyes told the whole story. The South Korean soldiers, outnumbered by the enemy, were exhausted trying to hold back the North Koreans, who were well trained and supplied with weapons and heavy tanks by the Russians. The South Korean soldiers had no such weapons; they had no tanks. Many of the North Koreans that they had faced had seen fighting in China for the past three years. They were battle-hardened and most just considered this an extension of the Chinese war.

Smith's group reached its destination a few miles north of Osan about 3:00 AM on July 5th, tired, cold, in the rain. A little later that morning, eight T-34 tanks were spotted, heading right toward our troops. The tanks were followed by a long line of infantrymen which was followed by yet another 25 tanks. The enemy column was later estimated to be about six miles long. Police action, my ass! This was a full-fledged war coming straight at them.

Our troops needed big tanks, big enough to take on the enemy's huge Russian T-34 tanks! We needed more jeeps, larger weapons, more ammunition, more men, and we needed them now! We needed some of the $21 million of military equipment that the US had committed to provide South Korea months before the invasion, military equipment that was said to be en route, and we needed it now!

When the enemy closed in within a mile, the Americans started firing their mortars. There were a few hits but the enemy kept coming. When the enemy was only about 700 yards away, the Americans fired their recoilless rifles, but the tanks kept coming. Then the bazookas failed to stop the enemy.

When SGT Loren Chambers of B Company of the 21st Regiment called for some 60mm mortar fire, the answer was that they wouldn't reach that far. When Chambers asked about the 81mm mortars, he was told that they didn't come with them. He asked for the 4.2 mortars, and was told that they wouldn't fire. "How about the artillery?" Chambers asked, only to be told that the Air Force didn't know the location of the Smith group.

Did his support fellow military people not understand that this small group of American soldiers was in grave danger of being overrun by the enemy who had hundreds of men and at least 33 tanks? Did they not understand that this small group had no defenses against the enemy? They needed help and they needed it now!

Finally, a frustrated Chambers sarcastically asked for a camera. When his support people asked him what he was going to take a picture of, he replied, "I want some kind of record of this as we all lean over and kiss our asses good-by."

Chambers, a veteran of WWII, had already earned five purple hearts. Within minutes after his radio contact with his support unit, Chambers earned his sixth.

Under the circumstances, the US troops had no choice but to fall back, and fast. Some took off their boots so they could move faster through the rice paddies. Some threw down their heavy weapons which they knew would only slow them down. There was no virtue in staying to fight when they had no weapons, or worse, stay and be captured and tortured daily or executed. I have a personal philosophy about fighting which I taught my children, Dawn and Derek, many years later: "Don't fight if you can't win; leave, and come back another day when you can."

Early in the morning of July 6th, after retreating several miles, LTC Smith could account for only 250 of the original 540 soldiers who had followed him into battle and the artillery was missing five officers and twenty six men. Other surviving soldiers of the

21ˢᵗ Regiment retreated to several Korean towns; some retreated to the east coast and reached the Yellow Sea and the Pusan port. Task Force Smith was supposed to show an arrogant display of strength to stop the enemy from advancing south. Sadly, the In Min Gun had been delayed only seven hours by Smith's men and many lives had been lost in the process.

Many critics were not complimentary of Smith's performance and said that his unit provided little or no resistance to the enemy. Truman, however, obviously did not agree with the critics. Task Force Smith veterans were honored by President Truman, along with Secretary of the Army, Frank Pace, at the White House in June 1952.

Chapter 8

—⁂—

New Commanders

Pharis' new unit, the 34th Regiment, was the next one of the 24th Division to face the enemy. He traveled by train across the large island of Japan on his way to Korea and passed through Hiroshima where the US dropped the first atomic bomb on August 6, 1945. Even after five years, the magnitude of the destruction was still there. Pharis saw huge pieces of metal burned into other metal pieces; he saw outlines of human beings in front of buildings where they had been standing when the bomb hit. Although many American lives had been saved by using the atomic bomb to stop the war, Pharis was saddened by all the destruction that had been left behind. Soldiers of the 34th boarded ships to be transported to South Korea and traveled in trucks to Taejon.

None of Pharis' enlisted buddies from his original unit had been re-assigned with him and he found himself surrounded by strangers. The first soldier whom Pharis befriended was an Italian man from the steel mill town of East McKeesport, PA, named Timothy Reza. He was only sixteen years old and looked like Charles Bronson. He was shorter than Pharis and reminded Pharis of his younger brother Bill.

Pharis, now 18 years old, took Reza under his wing and they became instant friends.

All of Pharis' commanders were also new to him. They included LTC Harold (Red) Ayers who had a fine record in Italy, 2LT Cordus Thornton from Dallas, TX, MAJ John J. Dunn, Operations Officer of the 34th Regiment, and MG Dean, Commander of the 24th Division. Dean's orders to the 34th's commander, LTC Harold Ayers, were simple and straightforward: deploy his men in blocking positions across the key routes southward at Ansong and Pyongtaek.

Our troops were short on men so the South Korean civilians helped carry the ammo across the mountains. The problem with accepting their help was that the enemy looked just like our friends in South Korea; our soldiers couldn't tell them apart. The North Koreans, on the other hand, knew exactly what their enemy looked like: mostly white boys from a spoiled and presumptuously entitled country. Some of the enemy disguised themselves as South Korean farmers, sneaked behind our troops, and attacked them from the rear. Many of our Americans lost their lives that way, when we misguidedly trusted the enemy.

The 34th Regiment had established its headquarters not far from Smith's forward unit. A small reconnaissance force was sent north and came back with news of tanks south of Osan. Later four survivors from Task Force Smith stumbled in at the 34th's command post and told of the enemy's attack on them and the number of North Korean soldiers and enemy tanks. Pharis' new commander, LTC Ayers, didn't buy it. He thought that these reports had to be wrong. When Ayers and his troops spotted soldiers coming at them, they rationalized that it must be some of Smith's men withdrawing down the road. When they realized that Smith didn't have that many men and he certainly didn't have any tanks, they knew the enemy was bearing down on them. It was just as Smith's men had described their encounter with the enemy to Ayers.

The classic signal came that the enemy was near when an endless parade of refugees was fleeing southward, trying to outrun the In Min Gun. It was soon realized that a large number of South Korean soldiers, outnumbering the peasants, was also fleeing southward shouting "Tanku! Tanku!" They had to mean that North Korea tanks were coming; our troops certainly didn't have tanks.

All too soon two T-34 tanks showed up. The Russian tank was perhaps the best all-around tank developed in World War II, with very high mobility, a good low silhouette, and very heavy armor plating. It could be stopped, but not with the ancient equipment in the hands of the South Korean Army, nor the Task Force Smith, nor the 34th Regiment.

As the T-34 tanks approached our troops, the American bazooka men moved in as close as possible and fired away, only to see their shells bounce off the tanks. The 34th US soldiers, like the 21st soldiers, didn't have any weapons to fight the enemy so their only option was to retreat, or stay and be shot, or worse, be captured. They chose to retreat in hopes that they would live to fight another day.

The enemy tanks kept coming south. By dawn, July 6, the tanks were in Pyongtaek, five miles down the road. Then they were in Songwan, and then they had advanced to Chonan, 36 miles in 36 hours.

That same day, when MG Dean heard that the 34th Regiment had retreated to a location south of Chonan, he was furious. He immediately turned his jeep toward their location. When he arrived, he demanded to know who had authorized the retreat because he certainly had not given the order. Dean had not considered that few of the radios worked in the rain and telephone wires were repeatedly cut, causing a total lack of communication between him and his troops. He was not aware of the enemy's forces and their sheer devastating aggression. Still, in

Dean's mind, he felt that the 34th, under the command of LTC Ayers, had not offered any significant resistance to the enemy and expressed his disgust with their lack of performance.

Dean screamed at the troops, "You cowards, you are a disgrace! Get back there and fight like soldiers!" Pharis remembered his principal in high school yelling at him over something that he can't remember now. He thought as the principal was yelling at him, "I'm just a poor boy from the country. Where I come from, no one yells at anyone else like this." He remembered that he had been yelled at in basic training which was normal but, under no circumstances, had anyone ever called him a coward. Pharis couldn't wrap his mind around the screaming and name calling. Didn't MG Dean understand that they fought as well as they could without any sufficient weapons to hold the enemy back? Didn't Dean understand that it would have been fruitless to try to hold the enemy back when they had tanks and we didn't? Dean's words still ring in Pharis' ears today and he has never forgotten the harsh, unjustified allegations shouted at them by MG Dean that day.

Dean thought that he needed an officer with more backbone to command the 34th Regiment and he promptly relieved LTC Ayers of his duties. He replaced him with COL Bob Martin, an officer with more experience of regimental command who had served with Dean in World War II. Martin had come to Korea at Dean's personal request. Dean knew that he could count on Martin to stand up to the enemy. He had witnessed his courage and bravery before. He knew Martin wouldn't let him down. Pharis now had yet another new commander to follow but he wouldn't get much of a chance to get to know him.

When COL Martin took over his new command of the 34th Regiment, he knew that he had not yet earned the respect of these soldiers. He also knew there wasn't enough time to get acquainted with his troops so they would follow him into battle. Even so, he knew that he had to find a way to pull the 34th Regiment together so they would fight as a team. Martin decided that his best option to get them motivated was to set the example of bravery himself.

Trying to defend the town of Chonan, COL Martin took a small group of about 80 soldiers inside the town. Martin and the few men who agreed to follow him found themselves involved literally in a street fight with the enemy. Finally, the showdown was between Martin's 2.36" bazooka and the North Koreans' 85mm shell from a T-34 tank. Martin fired his rocket launcher which fizzled out as it made contact with the tank's steel hull. At the same time the tank fired back at Martin. At a range of less than 25', the 85mm shell literally blew Martin into two pieces. The new commander of the 34th, following Dean's orders, had survived only 48 hours after taking command of his new unit.

On July 8, MG Dean received the news that COL Martin and some of his men were cut off inside the town and that North Korean tanks were in the city. Martin and most of the others were killed that day. Dean felt remorse that he had asked his friend Martin and his troops to go into a situation without knowing the full danger he was putting them in. He had sent his friend and many brave soldiers to their deaths.

After their commander Martin died, the resistance to the enemy had disintegrated and the troops started retreating. The two options left for the American soldiers were either retreat and be chastised by MG Dean or stay and be butchered by a superior and better-armed enemy. Without weapons to defend themselves, they had no other choice but to retreat.

The Americans who had been fighting in Chonan were concerned about being taken prisoners but were more concerned about the way they might die, in a most humiliating manner. The reports received after Smith's 21ˢᵗ had been overrun by the enemy confirmed the North Koreans' treatment of our soldiers. Some of Smith's men had been found with their hands tied behind their backs and shot in the backs of the heads. They had heard that it was not the enemy's policy to take prisoners. It was easier to just shoot them.

Later, when the American military and American civilians heard of the barbaric behavior of the North Koreans, they were shocked beyond belief. Their ruthless indifference to the treatment of our American prisoners caused a shudder of revulsion throughout our country. The news confirmed the reports that the soldiers were hearing on the battlefield; the North Koreans had no respect for human life, especially the lives of the enemy.

Chapter 9

—⚭—

Operation Delay Continues

Meanwhile, men in the 21st Regiment who had not flown in with Brad Smith were under the command of COL Richard "Big Six" Stephens, a compact, leathery veteran of WWII. The 21st Regiment was in a delaying position to the east, near Chochiwon. MG Dean told Stephens that his mission was to delay the advance of the enemy and to hold their position for four days.

Supplies arrived and Stephens was given an artillery battery, some engineers, and a company of light tanks. While any support was appreciated, our troops still didn't have weapons sufficient enough to stand up against the Russian T-34 tanks. Still they were just proud to get anything. The tanks they received were smaller than the huge and powerful Russian T-34 tanks but the soldiers were so excited that they cleaned them from top to bottom, a scouring that would pass any inspection. The soldiers even gave the tanks names, like Rebel's Roost. Knowing the superstitions of the Koreans regarding tigers, they painted tiger mouths with claws on their small tanks. The Russians had the advantage of heavier tanks, but our troops had the advantage of having sharpshooters. The Russian tanks were giants compared to our light tanks, but our tanks were giant killers.

One soldier reported, "We would fight, pull back, destroy the paths we left, set up again and fight again. Sometimes our outfits were actually winning; our troops were actually holding the enemy back, sometimes." They were able to hold the enemy off for a few hours, but when the North Koreans came at them, they came fast and from all directions.

The North Koreans gave our guys everything they had. Our troops responded but it was like one battalion (700-850 men) fighting against 40 tanks. The enemy not only hit them from the front, they also hit them from both flanks and from the rear. Another soldier said, "We would hide in shadows, trying to look like a hut or a corn field or a rice paddy. Concealment was our friend, but there were just too many of them."

With our troops being spread so thin and having to do double and triple duty, our soldiers were hurting, and they were beat up. They needed at least a week's rest but could only grab an hour break from time to time. Some went into the local streams and dumped water on their heads for a shower. Just letting their feet breathe by removing their boots was a luxury. They had to stay alert and ready at all times. Rest was never an option, not if they wanted to survive.

COL Stephens and his troops gave the enemy troops as good as they got, for a while. When the enemy approached, they were greeted with preplanned mortar and artillery fire which turned back the wave of the North Korean infantry. Then four enemy tanks moved out of a small village and started pelting the ridge where our troops waited with automatic fire. Stephens had no defense against that.

Stephens called for an air strike and, within minutes, the planes blasted the banks with rockets, but unfortunately without visible effect. The rockets were, however, effective in scattering the enemy's infantry. All too soon though the planes expended their ammunition and were forced to leave the area. Stephens' request for artillery did more damage than good. Enemy fire had destroyed the wire for their radios and communication with the artillery had been cut off. Thinking that the ridge had been overrun by the North Koreans, the US artillery started firing on the very ridge where Stephens and his men were positioned.

As much as Stephens wanted to obey the orders given by MG Dean to maintain his position on the ridge, he soon realized that he would have to retreat. As they were leaving the ridge, two American planes dived down and strafed them. Not only were they under fire from the enemy, but their own fellow Americans were mistakenly firing at them too.

On July 12, COL Stephens radioed MG Dean to tell him that he had nothing left to delay the enemy and was being forced to withdraw to the Kum River. Stephens' orders were to hold the enemy for four days. He had already been successful in holding back the best of the North Korean Army for three days. Regardless of their circumstances, our troops gave up ground to the enemy only a yard at a time all the way back to the Kum River, forty miles southward. Stephens crossed the Kum River and, along with about 325 men, set up a new blocking position.

Previously on July 8, LTG Walton Walker, Commander of the 8th Army, flew into Dean's headquarters in Taejon with some good news. Walker, 61 years old, was a stubby, rugged, impatient little Texan who attended West Point. He had served as a corps commander under General George Patton in Europe during WWII. Now, he was responsible for all the UN ground forces in Korea. He reported to Dean that the entire 8th Army, all four divisions totaling some 48-60 thousand men under Walker's command were coming to Korea. MG Dean knew that until the 8ᵗʰ Army arrived, it was still the responsibility of the 24ᵗʰ Division to delay the communists' attacks and to carry out Operation Delay.

That same day, Dean sent MacArthur a message stating that he was convinced that the American military had grossly underestimated the North Korean Army, particularly their superb training and their advanced equipment. It would take, in his judgment, a miracle to hold back this formidable enemy who had obviously been planning this invasion for a long time. The enemy was organized and prepared. The Americans had been caught off guard and had not been prepared, let alone organized. You might say that America had been caught with her pants down, all the way down to her ankles.

In early July, MacArthur told the Joint Chiefs that he needed eleven battalions, about 9,000 soldiers, simply to hold the line on the battlefield. Back in America, the veteran Marines from World War II had settled back into civilian lives. Now they were being rousted from their comfortable homes to serve in Korea. Although, after World War II had ended, they had not joined the Marine Reserves, their old contracts with Uncle Sam allowed the government to call them back for active duty if necessary. And it was certainly necessary.

The Defense Department declared a requirement of 50,000 recruits in September, 50,000 in October, and another 70,000 in November. At the same time, Congress allocated $11 million for emergency defense.

Draft calls were on the rise and advertisements were posted everywhere stating, "Uncle Sam wants you, now, for the Korean War." In both Japan and the US, soldiers who had been convicted of relatively serious crimes and were on the way to stockades in the States, were given an opportunity to redeem themselves. They could fight in Korea and their records would be wiped clean. When the North Koreans struck, one officer stated, "We turned the vacuum on. It sucked up men from everywhere, behind desks, out of hospitals, from depots. We filled up fast."

In the beginning, there was talk of requiring six weeks of combat training for the new recruits, but in reality there just wasn't enough time. Then there was talk of ten days of training when they arrived in Korea, but again there wasn't time. The talk of three days of special training once the soldiers reached Pusan was also shot down: no time.

As the North Koreans approached even closer, the American soldiers arrived in South Korea directly from the States, drew their gear and were shipped to their combat positions. Most of them didn't even get the chance to zero in their rifles or to calibrate and test-fire their mortars or their machine guns. Without training and experience for combat duty, these new arrivals were more likely to become a large part of the increasing number of casualties in Korea.

For the troops retreating, the next area of defense to try to hold the enemy back was the Kum River, the first wide, deep, large river south of the Han River, which would provide a natural defense line. This great watery trench surrounded the city of Taejon much like a moat surrounds a castle. In between the city and the river, however, the terrain offered no additional defense.

Dean knew that they could not lose the Kum River to the enemy and he was determined *not* to lose it. If the Kum River were lost, they would inevitably lose Taejon. They couldn't afford to lose Taejon, because its road and railroads led to all of South Korea. Dean sent out very firm orders stating that they must hold the Kum River line at all costs.

On July 12, Dean ordered all the troops to cross to the south bank of the Kum. Their orders were to bury mines in the roads as they retreated and blow up the bridges behind them.

The 34th Regiment had started retreating after their Commander Martin was blown in half in Chonan. They had traveled fast, but still tried to delay the enemy. Pharis stated that, at one point, the enemy had overrun them so badly that they had to retreat 40 miles in one night in order to reach the Kum River ahead of the North Koreans. The 34th had to pull back so fast that Pharis had to leave three 60mm mortars behind. Then he found an 81mm mortar, but unfortunately he hadn't been trained on it yet. He knew he had to do everything possible to keep the enemy from overrunning them. Pharis quickly educated himself on how to use the larger mortar and started firing.

All regiments of the 24th Division had suffered great losses. Out of the 2500 men the 21st started with, they had only 1100 men left. The 34th had 2000, and the 19th had 2300. Counting the supporting troops, the total man count who crossed the Kum River and positioned to fight the enemy in Taejon was about 11,700.

The enemy had fought all the way from the Chorwon Valley and had taken its share of blows too. The units stood somewhere between 60 and 80 percent of its original strength, but they were still backed by at least fifty tanks. Any way that shakes out, it was obvious to everyone that the UN troops were in an extremely dangerous situation.

Being short of experienced men and the equipment to withstand the heavy Russian tanks was a type of military fighting that was not taught in any military school nor was it taught in any type of military training. Still, MG Dean had to work with what he had at his disposal. Along the great arc of the Kum River, he strategically placed the 34th Infantry on the left, the 19th on the right, and the 21st in a reserve blocking position on the southeast.

Back home, the Pentagon and newspapers reported the situation in Korea to be much better than the actual facts revealed. The reports said that the enemy's morale was cracking and that the UN troops were kicking ass. On July 16, 1950, *Times* magazine quoted GEN J. Lawton Collins, Chief of Staff, as saying, "In spite of their greenness, the troops had done an exceptionally fine job." The military and civilians back in the States did not recognize that there was a problem in Korea; once again everyone was in denial. If a problem isn't recognized, there is certainly no solution on its way.

On July 18, LTG Walker flew into Taejon. He had been assembling data on the Korean situation and wanted to know from Dean when and where the enemy was going to be stopped. He told Dean that he needed him to hold the enemy in Taejon for two more days; that would give the 1st Cavalry and the 25th Division time to arrive in Pusan and advance on to Taejon. Help was on the way! Walker knew that Dean was a fighter and he had every confidence that Dean would do whatever was necessary to give him those extra two days. Supposedly, Walker also told Dean that, if necessary to save lives, he could retreat before the two days were up. Then Walker flew back to his own headquarters at Taegu, above Pusan, where the enemy was not bearing down on them, yet.

The fighting was bad everywhere and our troops were always outnumbered. Sometimes it was two to one, sometimes five to one, sometimes twenty to one, but the fighting at Taejon was by far the worst of all. Not only were our troops outnumbered, they were also out-gunned, out-tanked, and out-flanked.

Over the next few days, an ongoing battle between the UN troops and the enemy troops drew great losses on both sides. Our troops still didn't have the weapons and tanks to withstand the enemy's equipment, but they still put up a tremendous fight.

There is no point in detailing the day-by-day, blow-by-blow actions that took place during those days. The actions were just a repeat of the other battles fought between the UN troops and the North Koreans. The enemy attacked, the UN troops defended, and then fell back. The enemy got into our troops' rear and cut them off. The UN troops disintegrated and saved what they could. The same story just kept repeating itself, over and over.

The total front, counting the bends and twists of the Kum River, extended for thirty miles. The Kum itself was 200-300 yards in width, with four eight-foot embankments. The water level varied from six to fifteen feet in depth. It was a formidable barrier for the enemy to penetrate, but it also had sandbars in some areas that made it easy for the enemy to wade across. Dean knew that, with the Kum's low summer water level, the river banks would not deter the enemy tanks long, and he was right.

Originally Dean's orders were to hold the North Koreans back for an additional two days, but our troops had held them for another three days. Still, the help that LTG Walker had promised after two days had not arrived and our troops were about to be overrun by the enemy.

Chapter 10

—ᘯᘯ—

POW's Captured

Just 25 days after the North Koreans invaded South Korea on June 25, 1950, they had our 11,700 troops surrounded in Taejon, South Korea. They had us severely outnumbered and there was no way out. Each time our soldiers tried to push out, to punch a hole in the enemy lines, they were faced with 70,000 to 90,000 North Koreans equipped with at least 50 Russian T-34 tanks. Tough decisions had to be made, and MG William Dean was the one who had to make them.

Dean ordered the men to get everything ready to fight their way out through the enemy lines. They had no other choice. Everything was gassed and greased and lined up in preparation to leave. The wounded men and as many weapons as possible were loaded on the backs of trucks to transport out. Until the time was right and the orders were given to move, our troops waited, in 100 degrees weather. There was no place to go until the time was right.

On July 20, 1950, Dean's orders finally came: move out, try to break through the enemy lines. God be with all of them. Pharis and a few other soldiers jumped into the back of a truck which was carrying seven or eight wounded men. As their truck progressed toward the enemy lines, they braced themselves for the fight of their lives.

Suddenly Pharis' eyes caught a glimpse of a bright light, a flare, coming at his truck. He knew that this could only mean big trouble. He tried to jump from the truck but there just wasn't enough time. An enemy's bazooka shot his driver and blasted all the others out of the back of the truck.

Totally stunned by the blast, Pharis tried desperately to get his bearings. His helmet and rifle has been blown away and Pharis' survivor instincts told him that finding these had to be his first priority. Without these essentials, he had no defense against the enemy. He frantically searched as he crawled low to the ground until he finally laid his hands on both. He then realized that he had been riddled with shrapnel by the blast. He was bleeding profusely where the shrapnel had pierced his skin. The larger pieces had lodged in his left elbow and his right knee. He knew he had to treat these areas to prevent infection. Gangrene could claim his limbs, even his life. Maybe later. Right now he had to hide from the enemy. If they found him, he would most likely be shot again. He might not be as lucky the next time. The next shot could be fatal.

Pharis managed to crawl to a nearby irrigation ditch where he hoped the enemy wouldn't find him. Feeling somewhat safer behind the banks of the ditch, he took a few moments to tend to his wounds. He sprinkled the medical powder supplied by the Army on the bloody spots. Hopefully this powder would prevent infection; he could have the shrapnel surgically removed later. Pharis remained hidden in the ditch until he thought it was safe to keep moving. Maybe he could meet up with some of the other soldiers. As soon as he stood, he discovered that leaches, three inches and longer, had attached themselves to him. He was completely covered from his feet up to his knees. He tried desperately to remove the slimy pests but pulling them from his skin proved to be a very painful process. As they reluctantly turned loose, they left behind gaping holes where they had settled in expecting a long ride.

Pharis finally met up with seven other guys who were also trying to escape the enemy. As he surveyed the situation, he noticed that he was the only one who had retrieved his rifle. Not good. They all scurried around trying to find a proper hiding place, anywhere that they could be invisible to the enemy. They crawled through the infectious rice paddies that had been fertilized with human waste, any place to hide from the barbaric North Koreans.

All too soon, Pharis saw another flare. This time the enemy was using flares to light up the area to determine the exact location of our men. Once the enemy spotted Pharis and the others, they immediately started firing. They shot directly at Pharis and he should have died right then, but the bullet hit the rifle that Pharis had desperately retrieved and knocked it out of his hands. The bullet hit so hard that the impact caused Pharis' hands and arms, all the way up to his shoulders, to remain numb for several hours afterwards. The fact that the bullet hit his rifle and did not penetrate his body was the first of many miracles he would experience during his stay in Korea. He had literally "dodged a bullet" that day.

Some of the guys with Pharis were not as lucky. One soldier was shot in the back of the neck at such an angle that the bullet went down beside his spine, but he could still walk. Another soldier was shot in the gut but could still walk as long as he held his gut in. These guys were surrounded by the enemy; there was no place left to run. These eight soldiers were now the property of the North Korean military and all of them were terrified of what might happen to them next.

Winston Churchill was quoted as saying about the captivity of a prisoner, "You are in the power of the enemy. You owe your life to his humanity, your daily bread to his compassion. You must obey his orders...."

Pharis and the other soldiers had heard the stories about the treatment the North Koreans dished out to anyone they captured. The Communists proved ruthlessly indifferent to taking prisoners. They had no humanity. They had no compassion. Instead, they bound the captured ones' hands behind their backs, forced them down on their knees, and shot them in the backs of their heads, execution style. This barbaric act stripped the soldiers of all their pride and hope of ever surviving to see their loved ones again. This inhumane act minimized our soldiers to insignificant hollow bodies. Pharis didn't have any reason to believe that his destiny would be any different than that of his fellow soldiers who had already been shot. He had no reason to believe that he would be more fortunate than them. He had no reason to believe that his life would be spared. He expected to be shot just like the ones before him. He knew that the people back home, especially his mother, had been praying for his safety because he could feel it. While he appreciated their prayers, it seemed that his execution on July 20, 1950 was a done deal.

The North Koreans lined up the newly captured soldiers and aimed their machine guns at them. It reminded Pharis of the firing squads that he had seen in western movies. As they set their sights on Pharis, he thought of the family that he had left behind. Pharis remembered the fun that he and his sister Toot, now 15 years old, had before he left home. She was always throwing something at him to get his attention, whether it was dried cow paddies or hard cotton bolls, which always led to his chasing her down to punish her.

He remembered Bill, his 13 year old brother, and all the times they got into trouble together, like the time they tried to teach some puppies to swim, in a frozen lake. They weren't going to make the puppies swim alone. They had planned to go into the water too so they had stripped off all their clothes. When Mama found them and saw what they were up to, she broke off a switch from a nearby bush. As she marched them back home, still naked, she struck their bare cold legs with each step they took.

It was the two youngest siblings, Butch and Helen, just seven and four now, who concerned Pharis the most. They were so young when he left that they might not remember him when they got older.

The face of his hard-working, gentle, loving father for whom he had a great deal of respect and admiration came into Pharis' view. Dad would be crushed; he would feel responsible for Pharis' demise. What a guilt trip to lay on anyone!

Last but certainly not least, he saw the face of his sweet, loving mother, and knew that this would probably destroy her. She loved all her children but Pharis was her first born child; she had loved him longer. She might not ever recover from this. She had begged him not to join the Army. Why hadn't he listened to her? As he thought his life was about to end, he talked to his mother. He said, "Well Mama, what are you going to think about this?"

It was the first time that Pharis had been put in front of a firing squad and, for reasons that we still don't know today, the enemy did not follow through with the threat to shoot him. The reputation of the enemy was to take no prisoners, especially those who were wounded like Pharis. This was the second miracle for Pharis in just one day.

The North Koreans first stripped the American soldiers of their dog tags, making it impossible for them to be identified in the future. They took their clothes and their boots which they kept for themselves, leaving our soldiers with only their summer pants and t-shirts. Some of their boots were replaced with Korean canvas shoes which were too small for the larger Americans so their heels hung out over the backs of the shoes. Pharis was not one of the fortunate ones who got the smaller shoes. Why waste shoes on a wounded man when he probably wouldn't last long enough to enjoy them? He was left with only his socks to walk over the rocky Korean terrain.

The North Koreans ordered the new POW's to start walking north toward Seoul. The pain from his wounded knee made it almost impossible to walk but Pharis knew that he would certainly be shot if he couldn't walk. He had to fight the pain and find a way to keep moving. He had already experienced two miracles today. He knew the prayers from back home were working, but he couldn't risk pushing his luck any farther. He had to walk!

Pharis, now just 18 years old, had no concept of what the next 37 months would hold for him but he knew it would be the toughest challenge he would ever face, if he survived. He didn't know if his captors would allow him to survive. They could decide at any time to shoot him, especially because of his wounds. For the most part, the enemy held his fate in their hands.

Pharis would reveal some 45 years later that he had a dream, long before the date of his capture, that he would spend many years in a prison camp. That dream had become a reality on July 20, 1950. This was only one of the many dreams that Pharis would experience about his future.

On the morning of July 20, after almost all of the UN troops had left Taejon trying to break through the enemy lines, MG Dean heard heavy gunfire as the ragged line his troops had drawn around Taejon grew smaller and smaller. The city was now on fire and he heard the North Korean tanks, now inside Taejon. Since he hadn't been able to make contact with his troops, for the first time in weeks, MG Dean had no command decisions to make. He remembered that the new 3.5" bazookas had been flown in from the States. These bazookas were said to be designed to stop any known armor, even the T-34 tanks. He decided to go tank hunting. He wanted to see if they finally had anything that would stand up to the enemy even though it was too late to help the men of the 24th Division now.

Dean found a soldier with the new bazooka. He and a few others were able to sneak up behind a tank, but the tank turned around and started toward them. The bazooka man took aim, but he was shaking so hard that he blew up the street a few yards in front of them. He had only one round of ammunition so another chance of taking the tank down was spoiled.

As the T-34 tank waddled toward them, and then *past* Dean and the others, Dean was so infuriated that he pulled out his .45 automatic and emptied the magazine at the tank as it passed by him. The .45 automatic proved to be no threat to the tank as the bullets bounced off it.

Then hundreds of North Korean soldiers, disguised as farmers wearing white robes, infiltrated the city. Once in, they stripped off their white robes, revealing their enemy uniforms and opened fire on the remaining UN troops. The snipers were everywhere, firing from the building tops and even from the trees.

Later that day, Dean found another bazooka man but this one had more than one round of ammunition. They decided to find another tank to attack. Along the way, they dodged sniper fire but they fired back, taking out a few snipers themselves. The North Korean infantry had one particular tank covered so Dean and his bazooka man had to climb up to a second floor of a house to get a good shot at the tank. When they peeked out the window, they were faced with the muzzle of the tank's 85mm pointed directly at them. Dean instructed the bazooka man to fire and he did. A sharp, excruciating yell came from the tank. Dean said, "Hit 'em again!" When they hit the tank for the third time; the horrible screaming stopped and the tank started to smoke. At least one tank was down. It was time to go.

Most of our troops had evacuated the city of Taejon earlier. Dean and a few others who had remained behind caught up with a convoy as it was being ambushed, trucks burning along the road and sniper fire smacking the pavement all around. As their jeep rushed through the maze of turmoil, they were driving so fast that they missed their turn, a road that could have taken them to safety. The jeep crashed. The surviving MG Dean, stunned by the impact, started wandering around aimlessly trying to find his way to his troops. After a few days of being lost, Dean was captured by the enemy and kept in isolation during his 37 months in captivity.

Those who got out of Taejon were heroes. Those who did not were heroes. There's just no better word to describe these brave and fearless soldiers. Without the extra days MG Dean had given LTG Walker at Taejon, the final defense of Pusan probably would not have been possible. Overall, had it been worth it? At best, the Americans had merely slowed down the ferocious drive south by the North Koreans by a few days, but that delay had been at a tremendous cost to the US and the South Korean armies. In the first week, not only had the North Korean army destroyed most of the South Korean army (those who weren't able to flee), they had also virtually destroyed three American regiments. Some 3,000 men were either killed, wounded, or missing in action, and enough weapons had been left behind by the Americans and the South Koreans to outfit one or two North Korean regiments.

Chapter 11

—ᴍ—

The Pusan Perimeter

The American troops who were successful breaking through the enemy lines at Taejon were still being hounded by the enemy, but they had a mission to complete: Operation Delay. The US troops kept up their routine: fight, pull back, destroy the roads and bridges that they just left, set up and fight again until they reached the Naktong Line. That area became known as the Pusan Perimeter, the last place left for the UN troops to take a stand against the enemy.

The Pusan Perimeter was surrounded by the Naktong River on the peninsula, and the Korea Strait and the Sea of Japan on the coast line. Behind the Naktong River, the area was a rectangular box of terrain ranging about 130 miles from north to south and 50 miles across. It had cover on the west with the barrier Naktong and high and rugged mountains across the north. If our troops couldn't stand their ground there, they would be forced into the sea. They could *not* be defeated. Once they arrived at the Pusan Perimeter, there was no other place to retreat.

There were many battles fought during the retreat to the Pusan Perimeter. The North Koreans were advancing not only from the north, but they were also coming at our troops from the west. A North Korean division had hooked around Taejon and hastened through the defenseless countryside southward. If the North Korean soldiers reached Pusan first, our troops would be encircled with little chance to escape. LTG Walker rushed to send units of the 25th Division down to Masan to block the advance of the North Koreans.

In seventeen days of combat, the 24th Division had been driven back one hundred miles and lost enough materials to equip a full-strength infantry division. Second only to the Soviets, the American Army became the principal supplier to the North Korean army's In Min Gun of guns and ammunition.

Our troops were outnumbered and out-weaponed and the American military and government back in Washington began to fear that our troops would not be able to hold the enemy back. Once again the atomic weapon was considered in order to contain the enemy.

In the last days of July, LTG Walker began to issue a warning order. Once they reached the new defensive position behind the Naktong River, he stated profoundly, that there would be no more retreating, withdrawal, readjustment of lines or whatever they might call it. There were no lines behind which they could retreat. A retreat at Pusan would result in one of the greatest butcheries in history. They must fight to the end. They must fight as a team. He stated that, if some of them died, they would die fighting together.

As the confidence of LTG Walker and his army reached an all-time low and they thought that defeat was inevitable, hope showed up. Replacements, tanks, and weapons had arrived in Pusan during the latter days of July. These new troops smiled and walked differently, much like the ones who had arrived with the 24th Division some weeks ago. These new outfits were fresh and ready to shoot. Artillery firing sounded like music to everyone's ears and the morale increased by 100%, for a while.

Now our troops had a little more power to put pressure on the enemy and give it to them steady. This was payback time for the North Koreans. Still, the attacks from the enemy never let up. Some of the strongest attacks from them came from small patrols which could move faster and surprise our men with their relentless efforts.

In spite of all the UN losses, the UN troops actually outnumbered the In Min Gun with the arrival of the new soldiers. It was the first time that the UN had this advantage and one that they would never lose again. It was discovered later that the North Koreans had suffered some 58,000 casualties between June 25 and early August.

On August 1, Walker commanded an orderly withdrawal across the Naktong River, their last natural defense barrier. Once everyone had crossed the Naktong, the bridges were to be blown up behind them. By August 3, everyone had crossed over the river except one battalion of the 8th Cavalry, the rear guard. Their orders were to dynamite the bridge but they had to handle a huge problem before completing their mission.

Behind the last battalion, thousands and thousands of local civilian refugees clamored to seek safety across the river, to get to Pusan where they could hopefully get transportation out of Korea. Every time the rear guard rushed across the bridge, thousands of Korean civilians followed.

The final order to blow the bridge was to be given by GEN Hobart Gay, the division commander. Gay had been Patton's chief of staff in Europe and had never experienced the action of retreating in his military career. Gay instructed the rear guard to explain to the civilians that the bridge was going to be blown, take them back across the bridge and leave them there. Each time this happened, the refugees dashed madly for the bridge and totally filled it again. Three times this maneuver was repeated without success. Finally, realizing that the In Min Gun was getting closer and it was growing dark, GEN Gay had to make the toughest of tough decisions. He solemnly ordered, "Blow it", knowing that his order would be killing hundreds of Korean civilians.

Without a victory in sight, the Pentagon started questioning the effectiveness of the leadership of the American troops in Korea. The leadership from the Commander of the 8th Army, LTG Walton Walker, came under intense scrutiny. In early August, the Army sent its best officer, LTG Matthew Bunker Ridgeway, a young impressive forceful man capable of standing up to MacArthur himself, to Korea. Ridgeway, part of a high level three-man team, was sent to meet with GEN MacArthur to evaluate his needs and pass on the concerns from the Pentagon. What the special team found was appalling to Ridgeway.

Too many of Walker's key officers were older men who had *not* served well in World War II and were taking this last opportunity to serve so they could retire at a higher level of rank and pay. Ridgeway, like Walker, was furious about the quality of officers he was forced to accept. Walker had asked for some good officers but it was rumored that as soon as the good ones reached Japan, they were siphoned off and assigned to MacArthur's headquarters in Tokyo.

Although Ridgeway felt that Walker was a good and decent officer, he also felt that Walker was way in over his head on this assignment. Some of his Regiment Commanders, even though they were older, still lacked combat experience. Some of the troops were not up to the standards that America had enjoyed in World War II. Ridgeway thought that, if Walker could be given a tank unit and specific orders, he would be in his own element and he would excel.

The three-man team all agreed that Walker should be relieved of his duties; he lacked the larger command skills and the vision necessary to change. Even MacArthur had lost confidence in Walker and thought he should be replaced. All agreed that Ridgeway should be Walker's replacement. Ridgeway was, however, reluctant to replace Walker. He didn't want to add any more concerns to the already fragile morale of the troops. He also didn't want to appear to use his influence with Washington to become Walker's replacement.

Ridgeway asked Walker what he would do if the American troops were driven from the Naktong line. Walker replied defiantly, "I will not be driven from the Naktong line!" One quality that Ridgeway discovered that Walker possessed was his bulldog tenacity. Walker's unique attitude impressed Ridgeway. Ridgeway decided that Walker would remain in his position as the leader of these troops. Besides, Ridgeway's talents might be needed elsewhere if and when a bigger war started as a result of this "police action".

LTG Walker was determined to hold their ground inside the Pusan Perimeter and if necessary, he had committed to be the last man standing. Walker appeared to be tireless and fearless to his troops. At times he and his pilot would fly in his little reconnaissance plane, just a few hundred feet above the ground, almost daring the enemy machine guns to bring him down.

Some of the men thought that Walker was a psychic because he knew almost every time where the enemy was going to try to penetrate their line. He wasn't a psychic; he was a good listener with good eyes. He and his pilot flew over the In Min Gun's positions so low and so often that he knew a great deal about the enemy's troop dispositions and how much they changed from day to day.

If Walker thought his troops were even thinking of retreating or beginning to panic, Walker would instruct his pilot to fly as low as possible so he could have a little talk with them. The pilot would drop the plane to 300 feet, pull back the flaps, cut the throttle, and glide in just fifty feet above the troops. Each time the pilot hoped and prayed the engine would start again and their bodies would not be splattered all over the ground. At this point, Walker, a Three-star Commander of the 8ᵗʰ Army, would lean so far out the door that he was essentially no longer in the plane. He would scream through his bullhorn, "Stop! Go back, you yellow sons of bitches! Go back! You had great positions!"

Some would report that they had never seen fighting as bitter and relentless and raw as the many battles that were fought during the month of August at the Naktong River. Such was the battle over Hill 303, later named "Atrocity Hill". The 5ᵗʰ Regiment was deployed north to defend a sector that included the Naktong around Waegwan and the main road running southeast from there to Taegu. The enemy captured the UN troops, forty-five men, tied them with communication wire, and shot them in the backs of their heads. Only four survived this horrible massacre; forty-one did not.

Chapter 12

—∞—

Fellow POW's

The enemy ordered Pharis and the other men who had been captured to continue marching north. Their first destination: Seoul. At this point, the weather was still hot and humid. The summer uniform pants and t-shirts were all right for this type of weather.

Pharis had not been one of the lucky ones who received the small canvas shoes from the North Koreans. He was left with only his socks to protect his feet from the rocky terrain. As the marching continued, Pharis realized that he had developed large blood blisters on his feet and the pain from the blisters had become excruciating. Then the blisters burst and the pain got worse. At the end of the day, the blood had dried on his feet and socks. Pharis thought that he needed to investigate the severity of his blisters. He tried to remove his socks to see just how bad his feet were damaged. When he pulled off his socks, the dried blood came with the socks, exposing raw skin again. The pain started all over again. Pharis learned that it was just better to leave the socks in place, along with the dried blood. After a period of time, the dried blood served as a little cushion, like the sole on a shoe.

From the very beginning, there was never enough food for all the UN prisoners which would lead to malnutrition for all of them. North Korea was a very poor country without enough food to feed their own people, let alone feed their captured enemies. The North Koreans had become accustomed to eating less food with very little protein, but the captured ones would suffer greatly with this change of diet.

As the prisoners and their captors marched north, other groups of captured POW's from other battlefields joined them. Several people on this horrible journey would leave a lasting impression on Pharis for the rest of his life. Some of his memories are good, some are sad, and some are horrific.

The highest ranking officer in the group of the POW's was MAJ John J. Dunn, with whom Pharis developed a friendship. Dunn had seen tough times while a company commander with the infamous Merrill's Marauders who served in Burma during WWII and received the Distinguished Service Award. He shared with Pharis the details of the events that occurred when he was captured on July 7, 1950. He was the Operations Officer of the 34th Infantry moving north from Chonan with the 3rd Battalion of that regiment per MG Deans' order. During the confusion and chaos of being ambushed by the enemy and receiving incoming friendly fire, the 3rd Battalion began to retreat. Dunn reported the actions of the 3rd Battalion to COL Martin who had just taken over the 34th Regiment.

COL Martin believed the troops would take orders from MAJ Dunn and sent him back to stop the retreating. Dunn managed to turn the troops around and he quickly pulled out ahead of the battalion. Dunn was the first one shot. The bullet hit him in the jaw and blood spurted all over the road. Dunn fell out of the jeep and crawled off the road behind some bushes where he attempted to stop the bleeding. Due to the severity of his wound, Dunn couldn't attempt an escape to safety. All he could do was hope for a rescue by his own people. After a couple of hours of waiting, Dunn saw a large group of North Korean soldiers advancing down the road toward him. They found Dunn and several other wounded American soldiers and took them prisoners. Much to his disappointment, Dunn had not been rescued by his fellow soldiers.

Along the way to Seoul, Pharis met others who would become friends and whose friendships he would maintain throughout his time in a POW camp. He met Wayne A. "Johnnie" Johnson with the 21st Regiment, captured July 11th. Pharis described this soldier as a crazy man. He met Wilbert R. "Shorty" Estabrook with the 19th Regiment, captured on July 16th. Other friends included Jack Browning with the 21st Regiment, from Harlan County, Kentucky, captured July 8th near the small town of Chonan, and Jack Goodwin from Waco, TX. This small group of friends would prove to be each other's lifelines throughout this horrible experience.

The POW's arrived in Seoul about the third week in August, a month after Pharis was captured. The long march and the lack of food and water left the prisoners completely exhausted. The lack of water was the worst. The thirst was enough to drive a man crazy, crazy enough to drink anything, even drink from the filthy rice paddies fertilized with human waste. Some felt that they would surely die from a lack of water, if the filthy water didn't kill them first. As a result, everyone got dysentery and numerous other illnesses.

When they reached Seoul, the number of POW's now totaling about 600, they saw the damage that our air forces had done to the city. Our planes had been instructed to destroy anything that moved, especially the trains, and they were doing an excellent job of following orders. The enemy housed the POW's on the second floor of a school building that had been completely burned out. Our planes dropped bombs everywhere and one of our planes came down and strafed the building where the POW's were being held. About twenty of our men were hit. Some of them died immediately and two or three died later.

At that point, "Crazy Man" Johnnie Johnson decided that the families back home had a right to know what happened to their loved ones. Since the enemy had taken their dog tags, many of these men would not be identified and the families might never know if their loved ones were dead or alive. Johnnie felt it imperative that records be kept and he decided to take on that responsibility. Johnnie had a little stub of a pencil and he wrote down the information on a piece of paper that he had torn off the wall. Since he didn't know most of the other POW's, he had to compile the information from anyone who knew the ones who died. He recorded their names, rank, serial number, date and place of death, and any other information he could get.

Since our airplanes watched for any type of movement to wreak havoc on, the enemy decided to move the POW's at night so they would be less likely to be seen. The POW's were transported to their next destination sometimes by rail but mostly by marching. They arrived in the capitol of North Korea, Pyongyang, on August 24, 1950.

At Pyongyang, the enemy exposed the POW's to yet another form of humiliation. The enemy guards, now on horseback, paraded our troops, their hands bound behind them, through the city to show everyone the weak, cowardly prisoners. As they marched through the city, the guards constantly struck them, kicked them and spat on them, trying to break their spirits. All the while, the North Korean soldiers boasted to the local Koreans that they were definitely winning the war; just look at these ill-trained, unprepared poor excuses for soldiers that they had too easily captured. Pharis said that he didn't feel humiliated; his mind was on the horses that the guards were riding. He hadn't seen any horses since he had arrived in Korea and just wondered where the guards found them.

Over two months had passed since some of them were captured, but they were still wearing the same clothes, parts of their summer uniforms, that they had been wearing when they were captured. Most of them had no shoes and some didn't even have shirts. Most of the POW's had not been allowed to shower or even clean themselves since they had been captured.

Everyone had lost a great deal of weight from the many miles of marching and the lack of food and water. Many suffered from diarrhea, worms, lice, parasites, night blindness, dysentery, and malnutrition. Medical attention had not been given to any of them. It was up to each solder to take care of himself and his own wounds. By then, several people had died. Johnnie had new names to add to his list.

In Pyongyang, the military POW's met the 81 civilian POW's, ranging in age from one to eighty three who had been captured at the beginning of the invasion on June 25, 1950. This group included children, missionaries, one of whom was blind, diplomats, engineers, journalists, a doctor, a hotel manager, a Foreign Traders Exchange employee, and a widow. Two of these civilian POW's would forever be engrained in Pharis' memory. He met an English Salvation Army Commissioner named Herbert Lord who was over 60 years old, with a long white beard and a bad heart. He also met a very sweet but frail 76 year old Mother Beatrix, (Ann Marie) Edouard, Sr. for whom Pharis felt a great deal of respect and compassion. Mother Beatrix was from France and served as the superior of the Sisters of St. Paul Orphanage in Seoul. A matter of life and death would enter into his relationships with these two people over the following few months.

The POW's were again housed in a school building where they saw the beginning of the relentless strikes by the UN planes. With our front line troops moving closer and closer, the North Korean soldiers had to keep moving the POW's further north. It is believed that orders had been given to the North Korean army to prevent any of our POW's from being rescued at all costs. If they couldn't march and keep up, the prisoners were shot. Those who could march had to keep moving. No one would be left behind alive.

On September 5, 1950 all the POWs, both military and civilian, were moved to the train station and put in open animal railroad cars and coal gondolas. They lay down in the cars while our UN planes, not knowing that the POW's were inside, continued to strafe them. With the UN forces now breathing down the necks of the North Koreans, the POW's once again had to be moved further north.

For the next five days, the POW's traveled in railroad cars some of the time and walked some of the time, headed to Manpo. On one of the railroad cars, Pharis met another soldier that would also become his friend at least for a short time. By this time, all the POW's were sick with some illness or other, but most suffered from dysentery. When the urge moved those with dysentery, there was no controlling it. All of a sudden, this man trying to make his way to a window or any other opening came rushing past Pharis. As he passed, he sprayed Pharis and several others with his watered down feces. Pharis and the others had already experienced humiliation from the enemy, but not humiliation from one of their own. Pharis screamed at the man, "You shit on me!"

When everyone finally calmed down, Pharis realized that the man couldn't help himself, but it didn't make the experience any more tolerable. The inability to control those urges could have happened to any one of them, including himself, and then he would be the one being yelled at. After a while, Pharis started a conversation with this man named Vernon Stallings and discovered that they had quite a bit in common. Stallings' home town, outside Cliffside, NC, was just a few miles from the town where Pharis grew up. They lived in the same county of Rutherford. In spite of their shocking, and extremely embarrassing for Stallings, introduction, the two of them became close friends.

The tension between some of the POW's heightened as the conditions under which they lived worsened. Tempers flared and it appeared to be inevitable that something physical had to happen to relieve the tension and resolve their issues. Pharis remembered two of his buddies who always jawed back and forth and threatened to do each other bodily harm. Finally the anger between them reached the point that they both agreed to settle their differences once and for all with physical force. Both men grew up in the Midwest. One looked like a boxer and the other one looked like a haymaker so they were fairly matched in size. The two asked the North Koreans for permission to settle their differences in a pre-approved fist fight. The North Koreans agreed; they might enjoy some entertainment from the POW's. The fight was on. Pharis said that they both gave it everything they had. He had never seen that much blood anywhere before. When the fight was over, there was no obvious winner but the two never argued about anything again. After learning to respect each other's capabilities, they became good friends.

When the prisoners started walking again, the temperatures had started dropping and the cold winter months were just ahead. Pharis realized that a small fire would feel good when they would be allowed to stop so he started picking up sticks along the way to build a fire. Once when he leaned over to pick up more sticks, he was hit so hard in his derriere with the butt of an enemy rifle that he went sprawling to the ground, losing all his treasure of sticks that he had spent so much time collecting. It hurt so badly that Pharis was convinced that his tailbone was broken and he was concerned that the hit had caused some internal injuries. He had to resign himself to the fact that he would not have the warmth of a fire when they reached their destination. Pharis would experience the harsh blow of a rifle butt many more times in his future.

They arrived at Manpo on September 11, 1950, located at the Yalu River near the Manchurian border. The temperatures had plummeted and this winter was projected to be the coldest winter that Korea had experienced in 100 years. No one was dressed appropriately for the cold temperatures which would go as low as 50 degrees below zero. Everyone was still dressed in summer clothes and most of them didn't have shoes of any kind. Still, it could have been worse. At least they had shelter in deserted Japanese Army buildings, not outside in the snow and wind, but that wouldn't last long.

During the warmer weather, Pharis had contacted malaria and the symptoms had returned. He suffered from extreme chills and fever, unable to walk. The guards took him to a building where some of his fellow prisoners had the duty of taking care of the sick. They didn't have any medical supplies so they had to do the best that they could and improvise. There Pharis met a new friend, Johnny Eldridge, a man from Ohio who had been captured on July 8th. Johnny asked Pharis, "Did you come in here to die? If you did, just find yourself a spot in the corner out of everyone else's way and go on and die!" Pharis was furious! What an insult! Pharis had no intentions of dying and he would prove it to Johnny. That determination probably helped save Pharis' life, that and the prayers from back home. Another miracle. That day was the beginning of a lifelong friendship between the two.

The high fever that comes with malaria also causes tremendous thirst and Pharis asked a Lieutenant who had a canteen for one sip of water. The Lieutenant replied, "No, this water is just for me." Pharis had been taught all his life to share and to help those who couldn't help themselves, so he was hurt and disappointed at the Lieutenant's response. In fact, Pharis' health had deteriorated greatly because he had tried to help take care of others. In the end, that water didn't help the Lieutenant either. Not too long after Pharis' request for water, he had to help carry the Lieutenant up the hill where he would join the rest of the group of dead people.

Chapter 13

—⚹—

MacArthur's Own Agenda

As early as the third week in July 1950, when the North Koreans were driving the American troops back to the Pusan Perimeter, GEN MacArthur started planning Operation Chromite. It involved a very risky landing at the port of Inchon, located on the west side of South Korea near Seoul. MacArthur originally planned to use the 1ˢᵗ Cavalry Division but was told it would take too long to get the unit in place. With the rapid gains from the Communists, he had to go to Plan B; he decided to use Marines instead for this amphibious landing. If Pharis had *not* been re-assigned to the 24ᵗʰ Division as a replacement, he would have been part of the infantry who participated in the Inchon landing.

The narrow channel that the ships had to pass through and the high tides with limited hours for landing caused major concerns about the success of the venture with the Joint Chiefs of Staff (JCS). MacArthur explained to the JCS that if they didn't approve a plan to attack the North Koreans from the rear, the military at the Pusan Perimeter would have to continue to hold their position indefinitely or be pushed into the sea. The JCS knew MacArthur's reputation as an experienced and capable wartime leader and were finally forced to approve his plan. Still, MacArthur didn't want any surprises if they decided to change their minds. As insurance for this, he gave the JCS several other options for the landing point and didn't reveal that is was Inchon where he planned his landing until it was too late for the JCS to stop him.

UN planes participated in the conspiracy to not let the JCS, as well as the enemy, know where the landing was going to be. They bombed several other landing ports to confuse the enemy. At the same time, 260 ships and 70,000 men left Japan on the way to Korea. At 6:33 AM on September 15, 1950, the Marines hit the beach at Inchon and were met with almost no resistance. The enemy's military never suspected that UN troops would attempt such a dangerous landing at Inchon. Like the American JCS, the enemy thought such an endeavor would prove to be disastrous. In spite of the risks, 18,000 Marines landed that day and advanced 10 miles east of Seoul, with only 20 casualties. Within days, 50,000 Marines landed, MacArthur was ashore, and Seoul was once again liberated.

In a coordinated effort with the landing at Inchon, GEN Walker launched severe assaults all along the Pusan Perimeter. After three days of hard fighting, the North Koreans finally started to retreat. Walker and his troops broke out of the Pusan Perimeter and chased the North Koreans north on their way to meet up with the Inchon groups near Osan.

As our troops were quickly approaching Taejon, the North Koreans had to retreat to the north or be captured by the UN forces. Obviously there had not been enough time to get all of the UN POW's together and get them out of Taejon before our troops arrived. There were just too many POW's to move them quickly and yet they couldn't leave them behind to be rescued.

When our troops arrived in Taejon, they saw a sight that very few men have ever seen, or should see. They saw approximately 60 UN prisoners who had been forced to sit in a prison yard, again with their hands tied behind their backs, and shot. Later they discovered some 7,000 South Korean bodies in mass graves in Taejon. This horrifying event became known as the Taejon Massacre of September 1950.

A couple of days later, the UN troops arrived at the 38th parallel. The North Koreans had retreated all the way back to where it all started. If the UN forces had stopped at the 38 parallel, we probably could have ended the Korean "police action" and saved many lives, but the goals in Washington had changed. Now the US wanted to not only drive the North Koreans out of South Korea, the JCS also wanted to "rollback" communism by driving the North Koreans all the way back to the Manchurian border, maybe beyond. On September 27, 1950, the JCS authorized MacArthur to cross the 38th parallel. Truman did not disagree with their decision for fear that the political arena might view him as being "soft on communism" if we did not get total victory. The decision to continue north prolonged the war three more years and costs us tens of thousands of lives. This decision was later considered to be an *absolute military disaster.*

By the end of September, the US casualties totaled 6,000 dead, 19,000 wounded, and 2,500 POW/MIA.

Even though MacArthur had been given the authority to cross the 38th parallel and drive the North Koreans back to the Yalu River, some skeptics at the White House still had major concerns about the Soviet Union and China intervening should the advance north take place. In contrast, most of the White House, the State Department, and the Pentagon felt that the time for the Soviet Union to get involved had passed. They also felt that China would stay out of the war if they were assured that the UN forces would stop at the Yalu River and not advance into China.

Truman asked for a meeting with MacArthur at Wake Island, 18,000 miles from Washington, to discuss the concerns. Truman had never met MacArthur, whom he referred to as "Mr. Prima Donna". Maybe it was time to look the man in the eye. It's possible that Truman also wanted to share in some of MacArthur's spotlight after his successful landing in Inchon.

At their meeting on October 15, 1950, MacArthur, in all his cockiness, assured Truman that the Soviet Union and China would not get involved in Korea. In fact, MacArthur boasted to Truman that he would end this war in November and have everyone home for Christmas.

MacArthur dismissed warnings received through diplomatic channels that China would enter the war if the UN forces crossed the 38th parallel. In MacArthur's mind, these threats were not real and were only made because China had been greatly embarrassed by the turn of events in Korea. Truman left the meeting with MacArthur feeling assured that MacArthur had everything under control and the conflict with North Korea would end very soon, but he was wrong.

As early as August, 1950, China had begun to prepare for entry into the war. Even if the UN troops had not reached the Yalu River, some believed that China's leader Mao Zedong would still have intervened. Mao believed that American imperialism had to be contained and his intervention afforded him the opportunity to eliminate any counter revolutionary opponents in China.

The UN military forces continued to bear down on the enemy pushing the North Koreans back to the Yula River. The UN troops forged ahead at such a fast pace that the North Koreans couldn't move the POW's and stay out ahead of them. These barbaric creatures had no value of life, especially the lives of their enemies. Their only option was to eliminate the POW's because they couldn't afford to have anyone live to tell of the horrific treatment that they had endured while in captivity.

In late October, another group of some 400 UN POW's were being held in a schoolhouse in Seoul for several weeks until the UN forces closed in. The prisoners were forced to march northward to the capital of North Korea, Pyongyang. By the time they reached the city, there were only about 250 prisoners left. Some had died of diseases or wounds. Some had been shot because they couldn't keep up.

As the UN troops got closer, the prisoners were herded into open gondola cars like sardines, probably the same cars that Pharis and his group had traveled in previously. The train moved north until it stopped outside a tunnel near Sunchon on October 30, 1950. The train tracks had been destroyed by the bombs being dropped by the American planes and the cars couldn't go any further.

The prisoners were ordered to get out. The guards told the prisoners that they were going to be fed but there wasn't a place big enough to feed all of them at once. The prisoners would have to be fed in groups of about twenty each time. Each group that went into the tunnel to be fed was ordered to sit down. Immediately the guards opened fire on all the prisoners with their machine guns. The firing went on and on, until the guards thought that no one could still be alive, but they had to be sure. When the firing stopped, the guards went to each prisoner and stuck him with their bayonets to finish off anyone who might have survived. Out of that 250 or so prisoners, twenty-one did survive that terrifying ordeal to tell their stories. Some survivors played dead and resisted the urge to scream when they were stuck. Others passed out and weren't conscious when they were stuck.

It's a miracle that Pharis and his group of prisoners were not the ones in that tunnel that day. They had passed through the tunnel earlier. They could have been shot just like the ones who met their demise in the Sunchon Tunnel Massacre.

Chapter 14

—ⱳ—

The Tiger's Death March

In early October, less than a month after the POW's arrived in Manpo, about 400 Chinese soldiers or "volunteers" as they called themselves, showed up where our POW's were housed. They claimed the Japanese Army buildings for themselves and the POW's were forced out into the cold winter temperatures, without proper clothing, without shoes, without shelter.

On October 7th, everyone moved out again, this time down river to Kosan. Eight days later, they arrived at a place that the POW'S dubbed the "Cornfield" just south of Manpo. A week later they were marched about twelve miles to the south of Jui-am-nee. They left there on October 26th, headed back in the direction of Kosan. On October 30th, they arrived back at the "Cornfield".

While living in the open with temperatures already so cold, the men did anything they could to survive. Pharis remembered trying to hollow out even a shallow bed in the rocky ground where he and several of his buddies could lie down side by side to share their body heat. He said the real trick was to be able to dig deep enough so the wind blew over them, not penetrating their bones. Many of the POW's didn't survive those cold and windy days and nights in the open fields and "Crazy Man" Johnnie had many names to add to his list.

Pharis and the other prisoners thought that things couldn't get any worse than having to sleep outside in subzero temperatures, without warm clothing, no shoes, very little to eat or drink, but they were wrong. On October 31, 1950, the prisoners met their worst nightmare. He called himself the "Governor of the Chunchon Penitentiary"; his real name was Major Chong Myong Sil, but the prisoners quickly dubbed him the "Tiger". He was tall for a Korean, slim, and quick in his movements. When he walked, he leaned forward slightly, sort of like the way Colonel Klink walked on Hogan's Heroes. His features were the typical Korean features except for his protruding teeth and his piercing and shifty eyes. He wore a tight fitting uniform and had a pistol strapped to his side. It only took a second for Pharis and the others to realize that a maniac was now in charge of them, one who had no respect for human life. He had the power to determine their destiny at any time he chose. Some believe that the Tiger was the North Korean officer who gave the orders to kill the group of UN prisoners at the Sunchon Tunnel Massacre just a day earlier.

In the "Cornfield", Pharis and the others heard artillery rounds close by. From the sounds of it, our troops must have been within twenty or thirty miles of the Cornfield and they were closing in. With our troops gaining ground toward the north, the Tiger had to decide what to do with the prisoners. He liked killing so his choice was not difficult. The Tiger decided that killing all of them right now would eliminate his problems of having to move them across the snowy mountains. After all, the prisoners were so weak that very few would probably make the trip alive anyway. Why not just eliminate them now and save them and himself the trouble? The Tiger made his decision. He lined some 700 plus POW's up at the edge of a rock cliff and set up the machine guns in a crossfire position. He would shoot all of them and their bodies would fall over the rock cliff. The snow would cover their bodies and no one would find them until next spring. It was the second time Pharis faced a firing squad. He thought that this time it was definitely the end for him and the others; they were all going to be executed on Halloween.

Once again, Pharis thought of his family back home and wondered if their prayers would save him this time. Pharis knew that he had miraculously escaped death several times since he had come to Korea when so many others had not. Now he wondered if God had just one more miracle in store for him.

The POW's were still uncertain what was going to happen next when they saw Commissioner Lord, the translator for the Tiger, trying to reason with him. Lord was basically begging for the lives of all the POW's. After a few minutes, Lord was finally able to convince the Tiger to reconsider and allow the POW's to march north, away from our oncoming troops. Pharis believes that he owes his life to Commissioner Lord when he came to their defense that day, and to the prayers from home, and to his Lord above. Another miracle.

The Tiger agreed to allow the POW's to live for the time being, but they must obey his strict orders. Lord translated the Tiger's strong message to the POW's. The Tiger wanted everyone to know that he was in command and that everyone would obey his orders, or suffer the consequences of death. Everyone must march. No one would be left behind. They would be required to march sixteen miles the first night. If anyone could not keep up, including the elderly civilians; they must march until they died! That night marked the beginning of the "Tiger's Death March".

The march didn't start on time as the Tiger had planned. They didn't get started until almost nightfall. The Tiger obviously had a schedule to keep and this delay enraged the already psychotic Korean. He drove the POW's, including the elderly, without any mercy in an attempt to get back on schedule. The Tiger's inhuman pressure to "Bali! Bali!" (hurry!) was hard on everyone. The rigorous schedule, the lack of sufficient food and water, the lack of warm clothing and shoes, the subzero temperatures, and the snow were all contributing factors that caused many to fall out. It was especially hard on those who suffered from severe dysentery who had to stop numerous times to the call of nature and then hurry back in line with guards at their heels.

The Tiger forced the POW's to march until about midnight. Instead of the sixteen miles that the Tiger insisted they must complete, they had marched only about six. They stopped and spent the night in an open field. The snow wasn't sticking yet but it was extremely cold, especially with the wind factor. Pharis and some of his friends huddled together to try to find some warmth, but the ground was cold and wet. They weren't allowed to move around to keep warm so they just endured and prayed for morning to come. Some of the POW's didn't make it through that first night on the Tiger's Death March. Johnnie had to add more names to his list.

On the second day of the march, November 1, the attitude of the Tiger had worsened. He was angry that his schedule was delayed and he was determined to make up for the time that had been lost. As they left the field that morning about daybreak, Pharis noticed the naked bodies of several soldiers. When he asked one of his buddies what happened to their clothes, he was told that while the soldiers were dying some of the other POW's wanted their clothes. They hadn't even waited to make sure that they were dead before removing what they wanted. After all, they would be dead soon and dead people didn't need any clothes. Pharis recognized one of the naked men. He was his friend from outside Cliffside, NC, Vernon Stallings, who had shit on him in the railroad car. Stallings had died in the early hours of the morning.

As the march started, the Tiger insisted that the group move at a faster pace. More and more people started falling behind. The stronger ones tried to help the weaker ones along. Some were physically being carried and some were being pulled along with a rope. Two Russian women were carrying crying, cold, hungry babies on their backs, while holding on to their other children by the hand. They had to trot to keep up with the pace. Those who had been helping others or carrying others were too exhausted to continue and eventually had to stop helping. The Tiger was again enraged and told Lord, "No one must drop out. I will not allow it!" MAJ Dunn suggested that the prisoners be assigned to sections with an officer and a non-commissioned officer in charge of each section. Each officer would be held responsible for keeping everyone in his section marching. Pharis and Johnnie Johnson were assigned to the section under 2LT (later promoted to 1LT) Cordus Thornton, the officer in charge of the 7th section.

After walking for half a day, the Tiger, standing on a hill looked back and saw several men sitting beside the road. He was furious that the falling out had not stopped and ordered all the officers to the knoll right in front of Pharis and the other men in the 7th section He had to do something drastic to make sure that everyone knew that he meant business and obeyed his orders. He demanded to know whose POW's were falling behind, but no one stepped forward to take responsibility. Then Tiger screamed at all of them, "I'll kill all of you!" The Tiger was told that his own guards had instructed the men to sit down because they were too weak to go on but the guards denied they had given the POW's such instructions.

Again Commissioner Lord intervened on behalf of the officers. He stepped up to the Tiger to try to reason with him, begging him not to shoot the officers. The Lord's request enraged the Tiger so much that he pointed the gun at Lord and threatened to shoot him too. Lord ignored the threat and kept talking. Finally the Tiger relented and decided that he would spare the lives of everyone except the officer who had the largest number of those who had fallen out.

After calculating, the Tiger decided that 2LT Cordus H. Thornton with Pharis' 7th section had more men falling out than any other officer. The Tiger asked Thornton why he allowed this to happen. Thornton replied that those men who fell out were dying and to allow others to assist them would mean certain death for all of them. Pharis confessed that he and the other guys assigned to Thornton's section weren't doing very well at keeping up.

The Tiger said, "You deliberately disobeyed my orders. What happens to a man in your country who disobeys orders?" Thornton replied, "He would get a fair trial." Then Tiger turned to a group of his own soldiers, the same soldiers who had instructed the POW's to sit down, and asked, "What should be done to a man who disobeys the orders in our army?" They yelled, "Shoot him! Shoot all of them!" The Tiger turned back to Thornton and said, "That's the way we hold a trial in my army. You are guilty of disobeying orders." Thornton only replied, "That's not what we call a fair trial in my country. In my country we call that a lynching."

The Tiger tied Thornton's hands behind his back and offered him a blindfold which Thornton declined. Then the Tiger ordered Thornton to get on his knees. The Tiger walked behind him, raised the fur cap that Thornton was wearing which had been given to him by some locals, and shot him in the back of the head. The Tiger, Pharis remembered, used his automatic machine pistol which looked like a Luger and used a long clip. If the trigger were held down, the gun would continue to fire but the Tiger shot 2LT Thornton only once. Thornton's limp body rolled down the hill. Cordus H. Thornton died like a man, a soldier, never once begging for his life or showing any fear. He had the respect of every POW there that day. He was the first soldier to be executed by this mad lunatic who obviously enjoyed killing.

Pharis and some others were squatting beside the road less than 40 yards from where the Tiger shot Thornton. He saw everything. There were children and teenagers who also witnessed it all. No one should ever have to see anything so horrendous, especially at such an early age. No matter what the age of those who were there that day, needless to say, no one would ever forget it. That sight of Tiger's first killing since he had taken charge of these prisoners still haunts Pharis to this day. He still feels guilty that his failing health may have contributed to the execution of 2LT Thornton. How do you ever get over that kind of guilt? He was embarrassed and ashamed that his body wasn't able to stand the conditions in Korea and Thornton had paid the ultimate price for it. He vowed that he would make sure that he kept up from now on. He couldn't take it if he contributed in any way to anyone else's death.

Pharis wearing hat like Thornton wore

The Tiger put his gun back on his hip and called for Lord to interpret for him. He said, "I only kill bad people. You have witnessed the killing of a bad man." Then he instructed, to no one in particular, "Bury him!"

—◆—

At first, no one moved. Everyone was in shock from what they had just witnessed. The first one to appear from the crowd was a tall blond Sergeant from Pharis' same 34th Regiment named Henry "Hank" G. Leerkamp. The Sergeant had joined the US Army in 1939 at the age of 18 and had traveled extensively with the Army. He served as an anti-tank man, an armed guard aboard the USS Panama, a crash boat operator with the US Army Air Corps, and had seen battle during

WWII in Germany with GEN Patton. He was much more mature and experienced than most of these young soldiers who had never seen battle before Korea.

Leerkamp moved down the hill where 2LT Thornton's body laid. He started digging with his bare hands and sticks that he found. The ground was hard and rocky and the digging wasn't going to be easy. All of them knew that the Tiger was in no mood to wait for them to bury 2LT Thornton. A few others guys joined the Sergeant to help. They all agreed that this brave man deserved a more honorable burial but this was the best they could offer right now. They buried him in a shallow grave and placed rocks on top. Pharis remembered the entire process, in spite of the hard and rocky ground, took only five minutes to complete.

From that point on, Pharis and the others tried even harder to assist anyone they could in spite of their own failing strength. Litters were made to help carry the elderly and when the ones carrying them were exhausted, the elderly seemed to get a second wind which allowed them to walk a little farther for a while. This scenario was repeated over and over. Those who had faith in God, who continued to receive strength from somewhere, were an inspiration to all the POW's, especially Pharis. It just made him more determined to survive this ordeal, no matter what. The march followed the course of a river, winding between hills, and finally stopped in a field beside a farmhouse. The POW's once again stayed outside while the civilians were allowed to stay in the farmhouse. The Tiger told them that they should not worry about the ones who had fallen behind. He said that they had been taken to the People's Hospital where they would receive excellent care.

The Tiger pulled Lord aside and forced him to sign a document certifying that everyone who had fallen out, as well as Thornton, died of heart failure. Lord knew this wasn't true but he had no choice but to sign the paper.

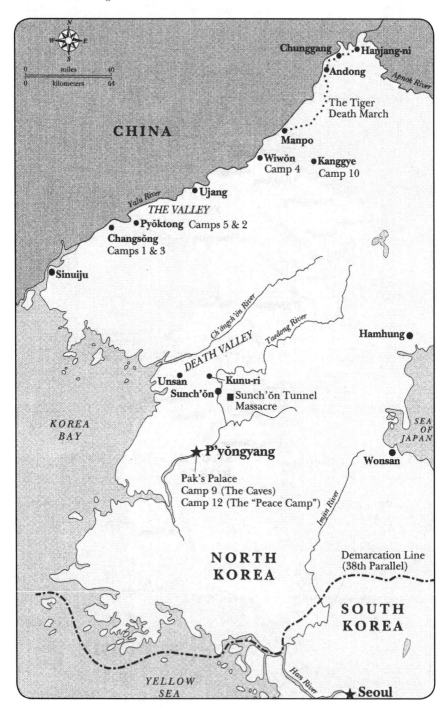

Pharis and the others had started putting straw in their summer pants and tying a rope around the bottom at their ankles to try to keep warm. They huddled together to gain warmth from each other. Some tried to get through to the fire that the guards had built, but they were driven back.

By the next morning, a dozen people had frozen and eight others couldn't walk. The Tiger speaking in Japanese ordered them to be left behind; they would be sent to the People's Hospital where they would receive excellent care. Pharis spoke some Japanese and knew that the Tiger was lying because the number the Tiger gave to the local people to bury also included the ones who couldn't walk. So much for the excellent care they would receive at the People's Hospital. As soon as it was safe, Johnnie added the names of Thornton and the others to his list.

November 2, the third day of the march, was another long day. The grueling pace set by the Tiger and the other usual factors left everyone exhausted. The elderly, even the 82 year old French priest, Father Paul Villemot, had all survived but were showing signs of failing health.

At the end of the day, they had marched another twenty miles with only a few stops to rest. The march finally ended at some school grounds where they spent the night. The civilians were taken inside a school building. The remaining POW's were crammed into a larger building but it still couldn't hold all of them. There were hundreds of freezing soldiers who were still outside. Finally, the pleas from those outside convinced the ones on the inside to jam closer together to make room for everyone, but the cramped positions of those already hurting from wounds, diseases, and the long marches, made everyone's pain worse.

The moaning and groaning and sometimes screaming, which the POW's obviously couldn't control, became so loud that the guards came in and threatened everyone. The guards told them to get quiet or there would be serious consequences, but the noise didn't stop. The third time the guards came in, they said, "This is your last warning! If we have to come back again, we will start shooting into the room as soon as we open the door!"

The senior ranking officer, MAJ John Dunn, knew that it was up to him to get control of the POW's or all of them would suffer the consequences. He told the men they would have to stay quiet for their own safety as well as the safety of everyone else in the building. Anyone who made any loud noises would be thrown back out into the freezing weather. For about 30 minutes, everyone remained quiet and then someone screamed out. Dunn ordered the officers and the NCO's to pass that person screaming overhead of the others and throw him outside. It got quiet again.

Shortly thereafter, another man screamed out. When the officers tried to pass him overhead, the screaming man fought back in order to stay inside. Then everyone heard a thud and the officer who struck him yelled, "Now throw him out!" The officer then gave his name, rank and serial number and invited anyone who so chose to file charges against him when they returned to the States. After that, it remained quite the rest of the night.

The following morning, November 3, and the fourth day of the march started just after dawn. The Tiger jerked open the door where the military POW's had been crammed together during the night. He ordered them to stand up and come outside, but only a handful of men could stand. The others had to fall out of the door or roll out until the feeling came back to their bodies.

After the POW's were given a small breakfast, the Tiger made a speech. He announced that his government was concerned about their health and ultimate release and they should appreciate everything that was being done for them. They should therefore cooperate in every way. They must all march with no more falling out.

Pharis' friend, Shorty Estabrook said about Pharis, "He always helped the others who couldn't help themselves and became weak because of it but he held on and kept the faith." Such was the case with Mother Beautrix. The elderly civilians were having more and more difficulty keeping up with the others, especially 76-year-old Mother Beatrix. When Pharis looked at her frail body and her angelic countenance, he was reminded of his dear Grandma Dobbins with whom Pharis shared a special relationship. Pharis was still running a fever from malaria, but he couldn't just leave her behind. She needed help. Pharis and three other guys quickly made a litter to carry her as long as they could before their strength failed them too. The guards watched this act of compassion but realized that very soon there would be five people falling out instead of just one old lady. The senior guard ordered them to put her down and leave her for the People's Hospital to pick up. She would get excellent care there. Pharis knew better because he had heard the Tiger instruct the locals before to bury the ones left behind and the number he gave them included some of the others who weren't dead yet.

Pharis and the other three guys refused to put Mother Beatrix down because they knew that the People's Hospital didn't exist. The guards insisted but the men held their ground and vowed that they would carry her all the way if they had to. Unable to convince the POW's to obey their orders, the guards changed their tactics of persuasion. The guards pointed their guns at Pharis and the other three and threatened to shoot all of them if they didn't put her down. Pharis remembered what they had done to 2LT Thornton and he knew the guards wouldn't hesitate to shoot them too, including Mother Beatrix.

Reluctantly, with tremendous sorrow, the four of them laid Mother Beatrix down. They realized that they would never see her again. They knew that she would never survive without their help. As Mother Beatrix sat on the ground, waiting for her demise, she gazed into Pharis' eyes, a look that still haunts him today. She knew she was about to die. He remembers a look that seemed to beg him *not* to allow this to happen to her and he is still riddled with guilt today for being helpless to stop it. He already felt responsible for 2LT Thornton's death. Even though I wasn't there, I am almost certain that Mother Beatrix wasn't dreading her fate, but more likely welcoming it. I believe the look she gave Pharis was telling him not to be sad for her; she appreciated this kind, generous young man putting his life on the line to save her, and she was looking forward to seeing him again in the future on the other side. They would celebrate their friendship at their reunion.

Mother Beatrix sank down on the ground; she could not continue on her own. Mother Eugenie, who was also exhausted, begged the guards to give Mother Beatrix a few minutes to allow her time to get her strength back. The guards weren't convinced that Mother Beatrix could regain her strength. They ordered Mother Eugenie to move on without Mother Beatrix but she clung to her until Mother Beatrix instructed her to leave, "Go, my sister, go."

As Pharis, Mother Eugenie, and the others were forced to leave Mother Beatrix and move forward, they all heard a shot. When they turned around to see what had happened, they witnessed the frail body of Mother Beatrix being pushed down a steep slope, rolling over and over and finally landing at the bottom of the ravine. On November 3rd, the day that I turned five years old, Mother Beatrix died, the first civilian to die on the Death March. With death comes relief. She was now no longer tired, cold, hungry or suffering in any way. She would go to meet God where she would be welcomed with open arms and receive the love and respect that she deserved but had not received at the hands of these cruel, barbaric, godless people.

Commissioner Lord was pulling the Russian widow, Madame Funderat, with a rope to help her keep up. After a short break, Lord once again started to pull her along. The guards stopped him and ordered that Commissioner Lord release her and leave her behind to rest for a while. Someone from the People's Hospital would be along shortly and she would be given excellent care. Commissioner Lord knew that the Peoples' Hospital didn't exist but he knew he had to obey their orders and, reluctantly, did as he was told. With great sadness, he untied Madame Funderat and left her behind. She was never seen again.

As the POW's marched north, they sometimes heard shots up ahead and sometimes passed guards who were laughing and joking around; there was nothing unusual about that. Climbing in the mountains became more difficult and they passed several POW's who were exhausted and couldn't go on. A guard stood beside each of them who had fallen out. After the group of POW's passed, a shot was always heard. The North Koreans were executing anyone who could not walk. Pharis vowed to make sure he could walk. Johnnie had to get more paper to add all the names of the ones who died that day.

When they were finally allowed to stop marching on the fourth day of the Death March, they had covered another 20 miles. The military POW's stayed in another schoolhouse and the civilians slept inside a church.

November 4, the fifth day of the Death March, brought new challenges to the already exhausted POW's. They woke up to a snowstorm. Steep mountains lay ahead that they had to cross before the pass was closed by the snow. Time was of the essence so they would not get any breakfast that day.

Certainly the wounds, diseases, and all the other factors played a huge role in whether the men and women and children lived or died. Pharis was determined to beat all odds and get back home to his family and friends. He decided that if God would get him home, he would never again give his parents anything to worry about. He would definitely straighten up and fly right.

Unfortunately, there were others who didn't share his determination. Some decided to take the path of least resistance and give up. For some of the POW's, it was just easier to die than fight to live. These were said to have the disease of "give-up-itis". They were the ones who had lost all hope of getting out of this mess and started refusing to eat. Even though there was little food and the taste was almost intolerable, everyone knew that anyone who did not eat would surely die. Next came the obsessive talk about anything, especially food. The blank stares came next. After that, it was just a matter of time before that man was found dead.

Pharis saw many men who had fallen out that day. He knew that they would be executed shortly. After seeing so many whom he knew would not last through the day sometimes made him feel discouraged and sometimes lose sight of his determination that he would be home someday, but somehow hope always came back. He hadn't suffered through his wounds, diseases, and the weather elements for no reason and he certainly wasn't going to give up now.

The ones who survived the snowy trip over the mountains and made it down the other side of the mountain pass arrived late in the morning on November 4. They were allowed to stop and rest at a schoolhouse in the Chasong village. It was the first place that had straw on the floor which made it a little more tolerable than what the POW's had been accustomed to. Transportation arrived that evening to carry the women, children, old men, and five very sick guys to the next stop. The others stayed behind where they got some rest until later the next day.

On November 5, day six of the march, the POW's were supposed to start their march at the beginning of the day. The rest that they received, however, just wasn't sufficient to revitalize them so they didn't start the march until that afternoon. Those who were able left together in a group; those who weren't fairing so well, left later. They only covered about ten miles that day and found shelter in another schoolhouse.

Day seven of the march, November 6, was much like the day before. Once again, the POW's left in two groups and covered about 10 miles. By this time, more and more people steadily got weaker and weaker. There were a greater number of POW's who had fallen out and were just waiting for their execution. As the ones who could still walk passed them by, some would ask for simple things like a cigarette but no one had a cigarette to give them. Another guy was lying in a ditch singing, "God Bless America" with tears running down his face. Some were lying still while their clothes and shoes were being removed, offering no resistance because they knew they wouldn't need them any longer.

Pharis was determined not to be one of those who had fallen out but his body wasn't convinced. His feet were worse and he couldn't remember if he ate anything yesterday. Did he remember to massage his feet last night after they had stopped for the night to prevent frostbite? He couldn't remember. By this time, everything was running together. He thought of the men who had been lost in the desert without water and started seeing mirages. He started hallucinating. He thought he saw his family and friends, but weren't they back home? Was this all just a dream or was it real? He couldn't remember. All he could remember was that he had to put one foot in front of the other and keep walking.

That night the prisoners stayed in another schoolhouse. When Pharis lay down to try to rest, he was petrified to see worms coming out of his mouth. He knew that the quality of the little bit of food that he received and the filthy water from the rice paddies fertilized with human waste couldn't be good for him, but this was ridiculous. As Pharis watched in shock as the worms left his body, he was terrified. These white slimy pests measured at least eighteen inches long and looked like earthworms but a lot bigger. Everyone had lice and hook worms from walking on the ground without shoes but these worms were like small snakes. They were obviously leaving Pharis' body because there wasn't enough nutrition inside him for them to feed on. They could do better somewhere else.

Pharis knew he had to do something to kill any remaining worms. He scrounged around in a closet in the schoolhouse and amazingly found a package with a small amount of arsenic in it which he swallowed. I'm not sure whether Pharis thought the arsenic would kill the worms or whether he was trying to do away with himself if he had to live with these worms inside his body. Remarkably, the next day, the arsenic worked on the worms and Pharis passed a ball, about the size of his fist, of dead worms. What are the chances of finding arsenic at just the time Pharis needed it to kill those nasty invaders? Another miracle.

November 7, day eight, was just more of the same. They marched. They stayed in a schoolhouse. That evening, MAJ John Dunn, the highest ranking officer, came into the schoolhouse with Commissioner Lord, and Dr. Ernst Kisch, an Austrian Jew. They wanted to make a list of the dead and missing. Kisch had compiled a similar list after WWII. They weren't aware that Johnnie already had a list.

On November 8, the terrifying and horrific nine days of the Tiger's Death March finally ended at Chunggang, located at the Manchurian border at the coordinates 41-45n and 126-52e. All those who marched and survived were merely skeletons of themselves; most of the men now weighed less than 100 lbs., a weight certainly not sufficient for the frame of someone like Pharis who is 5' 11".

The ones who survived had marched over 100 miles over steep mountains in snow blizzards and left 89 people dead behind them. The fact that anyone survived the Death March is indeed another miracle. When they arrived at their destination, everyone felt fortunate to be alive. Maybe now they could rest and try to get their strength back but the Tiger had other ideas. Being a fanatic about staying in shape, he forced all the survivors to do calisthenics that first night and the next morning. These men and women had hardly survived the march and now they had to find the will and energy to keep going. In the Tiger's mind, if they couldn't do calisthenics, he had no use for them. He might as well shoot them and be rid of the nuisances. For some who had contacted pneumonia on the Death March, doing calisthenics in the freezing November weather was the final blow. The numbers on Johnnie's list increased.

Chapter 15

—ᴍᴍ—

Life in the Prison Camps

The UN forces had advanced almost to Chunggang but they stopped short just a field away from the area where the POW's were being held. Pharis could see them not far away to the south. Everyone had hopes of being rescued but realized that if the UN forces came any closer, the Tiger would make sure that none of them would be rescued. They would be massacred.

The POW's stay at Chunggang lasted only a week. On November 16th, in the middle of the night, they were ordered to move out again. Just as they started to march, they were immediately halted and told to hide in the small surrounding buildings but there were too many POW's to fit into the spaces available. There was not enough room for 22-year-old PFC Jack Samms in the 19th Regiment, from Ashland, KY, Shorty Estabrook's best friend, even though Shorty and some other POW's desperately tried to pull him inside. Shorty witnessed the fatal beating of his friend, Samms, by the guards but Shorty was powerless to do anything to stop it. What a senseless waste of human life.

A short time later, they left Chunggang. That overnight march took them a few miles farther northeast to a small place along the Yalu

River called Hanjang-ni, where they would remain until the following spring. There was one large school building and several outbuildings where the POW's were housed. By the luck of the draw, some had the luxury of heat and some did not. Again, Pharis was not one of the lucky ones.

Their marching was over for a while but the POW's health conditions only worsened. Weakened by the factors that they had faced during their nine days of grueling marching and no medical attention, there was little hope of anyone's health improving. The many diseases and the unattended wounds caused such a stench that the guards had started wearing masks before they entered the buildings. The smell of death was everywhere.

Many of the troops suffered from severe frostbite that first winter. After all, they were all still in their summer pants, some with no shoes. Pharis watched as his fellow soldiers' toes and fingers turned black to the point that some could be popped off with just a snap of the fingers. Others lost their entire feet from frostbite. When he was asked why that didn't happen to him who had only socks to cover his feet, he replied, "I made sure that any time we stopped, I constantly massaged my feet, hands, legs and arms to keep my blood circulating." It's another miracle that Pharis didn't lose any of his body parts due to frostbite.

To make matters worse, the North Koreans didn't understand the POWs' diseases and which ones were contagious so they just threw everyone who was sick into the same room together, a place called the death room. Some of those who didn't have contagious diseases were then infected with something else. Even those with frostbite were thrown in with the contagious people. In that particular death room, there was no heat and the floor was bare, causing it to be even colder. The door to the room was sometimes nailed shut so no one could get out and the guards stayed away for two days. When the door was opened again, everyone was dead, or at least 99% of them.

Pneumonia and other severe respiratory infections wreaked havoc on many of the prisoners. Pharis contacted some form of a respiratory infection, maybe it was pneumonia, maybe it was typhoid fever which is an acute, highly infectious disease caused chiefly by contaminated food or water and is marked by high fever, coughing, intestinal hemorrhaging, and reddish spots on the skin. Pharis isn't sure which one it was. At one point, Pharis became so ill that the guards didn't give him any hope of surviving so they took him to a different room to die. He had heard the stories of the ones who never came out alive and Pharis was terrified. Once again, he thought his life was over. Pharis thought, "I'm just a country boy. I don't know anything about death and I don't want to know anything about death." The room was located above the kitchen where they did their cooking. The heat from the cooking probably saved his life. That little bit of heat allowed him to slowly start to recuperate. If the guards had left him where he was housed originally, without any heat, he would have surely died. Pharis became that 1% who came out of the death room alive: another miracle.

Due to a lack of enough nourishment, unless suffering from dysentery, everyone's bowel movements became irregular. Pharis remembers, of all things, that he went nineteen days at one point without hearing nature's call. Without medicine available to any of them, Pharis knew he had to find something to correct his problem or he would die. While rummaging around in a schoolhouse, he discovered a small bottle of Castor Oil, stuck deep in a corner on a shelf in a closet. Hallelujah! Someone back home was doing a lot of praying for him. The small bottle contained just enough to solve Pharis' problem and give him some relief.

Some of the POW's developed severe dysentery, a disease marked by diarrhea with blood and mucus in the feces. In the worst cases, a man's intestine would hang down inches below his anus, to be stuffed back with a surge of agony until the next call to defecate came. Sometimes those with the worst cases visited the latrine 30 or 40 times a day. Pharis became good friends with a man named Chris. Pharis valued their friendship so much that he named his only son, Christopher, after his POW comrade. Sadly, Chris never got the opportunity to meet Pharis' son; he died in the fields with dysentery, so bad that his intestines hung several inches below his anus.

During that first winter, in addition to contacting malaria shortly after he was captured, Pharis contracted jaundice, a disease condition in which the eyeballs, skin, and urine become abnormally yellow as a result of bile in the blood. He also suffered from rheumatic fever, an infectious disease that damages the heart, and beriberi, caused by a deficiency of thiamine, resulting in abnormalities in the heart and nervous system.

Pharis spent his first Christmas in Korea at the camp in Hanjang-ni. Unbelievably just one year before, his ship had docked in Japan. Excitement had overwhelmed him as he envisioned his bright future in the military, surrounded by these new places. How had he landed in this godless country, riddled with lice, suffering from diseases, wounded from shrapnel?

From the first day of Pharis' captivity, he could not allow himself to remember the past. Thinking of home and his family made it harder for him to adjust to this miserable life. He had to pretend that the days back home were just a dream; it never existed. On Christmas day, however, Pharis allowed himself the luxury of remembering, just this once. He remembered that back home did exist and his heart ached so much to see his family that he thought it would surely burst. He wondered how his family was celebrating the holiday. Were they laughing and singing Christmas carols? Was Daddy playing his harmonica? Were they eating oranges and apples and nuts as always? Were any of them acting in the church Christmas play? Were they having the usual Christmas dinner with turkey and ham and banana pudding and chocolate pies? Did they all miss him and wish that he were home or had they given up hope of ever finding him? Were they going on with their lives as if he no longer existed? Were they still praying for his safe return? God, did he ever miss his family and his home, especially on Christmas Day.

Pharis spent his imprisoned days gathering wood for the North Korean troops or working with the local farmers. The North Koreans traded the labor from the POW's in exchange for corn. The UN troops didn't get much of the corn, the majority of it went to the North Korean army. The POW's lived off of much less nourishment. They sometimes received a ball of grain, about the size of a baseball that they split among three people. Some days they received cabbage soup which contained only one or two heads of cabbage in a wash pot with several gallons of water and cane seed causing it to smell sour. Sometimes the North Koreans dumped the food in big troughs like the ones that the pigs back home ate from, except these troughs had flat bottoms. The POW's had their own personal bowl which they used to scoop up the food. The bowl became the POW's only treasure. Everyone had to keep up with his own bowl or use other means to get the food, even if they had to use their hands. Those who wanted to survive were not too proud to eat any way they could, with or without a bowl. It was just a part of survival.

Food was so scarce that Pharis and some of the others went to any extreme to get more to eat. At one point, when Pharis was housed in a hut with about 15 other prisoners, one of the men died. Since the amount of food that each hut received was based on the number of men in the hut, those who were still living made a pact. They all agreed to conceal his death in order to get his ration of food which they would all share. They were willing to keep a dead body in the hut with them in order to get 1/15 of his small portion of food. No one broke the pact but eventually they couldn't stand the stench that came from the dead body. They lost their extra ration.

When working with the farmers, Pharis and a few others sometimes stole an ear of corn for themselves and sometimes the farmers gave them corn. Realizing that they would be searched before re-entering the compound, they hid their treasure between their legs around their groin area. Luckily, the North Koreans hesitated to search the soldiers in that particular area, so they got away with it sometimes. Sometimes they didn't.

Late one night, Pharis and a friend of his from Hawaii faked the need to go to the banjo, the latrine. On the way there and back, they passed the bins where corn was stored. Of course, the POW's were never allowed to help themselves to the food at the camp. Both Pharis and his friend didn't believe that the guards could see them so they both quickly reached in and grabbed an ear of corn for themselves. They were wrong. The guards did see them and immediately commenced to punish them. Pharis and his friend were forced to get down on their hands and knees. One guard held a gun on them while the other guard started beating them with a bamboo stick that had been flattened like the sticks used to carry "honey buckets" from the latrine. Pharis was closer to the guard so he didn't get the worst of the impact but his friend who was farther away received the worst hits from the end of the stick. The guard beat them unmercifully until Pharis thought both of them would surely die. The end of the bamboo stick pierced his friend's skin and blood shot everywhere. The other guard hit Pharis in the mouth with the butt of his rifle and he lost his precious front false teeth, breaking them beyond repair.

When the guards finally stopped beating them, they pointed their rifles at them and Pharis thought once again that he was going to be shot. Once again, the prayers from back home were working. The guards didn't shoot: another miracle. They did, however, hit his Hawaiian friend so hard in the kidneys that they burst which resulted in his death later that night. All this over a couple of ears of corn.

Water was always very scarce in the prison camp. Even though the Yalu River was less than a mile away, the guards refused to allow more than one trip each day to get water. The water was brought in fifty-gallon drums on a cart pulled by some of our troops. Pharis remembered that there was one large Turkish man who pulled the wagon like a mule; he didn't need any help from the other guys. The North Koreans also used this large man to pull their plows in the rice paddies. Pulling the cart over the bumpy roads caused additional problems during the winter months. The water always splashed all over the ones pulling the cart. It immediately froze and the guys pulling the cart looked like some kind of monsters from the Arctic. With water so close, it was a shame that some soldiers who did not get water for five days died of thirst.

As the weather got warmer, they could at least move around outside and find other forms of food, rather than the hard corn and occasional watered down cabbage soup. They started catching and eating things that none of them ever thought they would eat. MAJ Dunn taught Pharis how to catch a snake, skin it, and eat it. He also showed him how to catch a frog and do the same. While some may think of these as delicacies today, Pharis had never heard of such a thing back on the farm, but he learned to love them.

Lice had always been bad in the past but with warmer temperatures, it became unbearable. They encountered lice in some rice sacks in the storage building as big as ticks and there was no way to get away from them. It became a ritual to delouse every morning if you wanted to live. Pharis and the others stripped off their clothes to shake out these pesky white invaders. As the lice fell to the ground, the POW's stomped them to kill them. They pinched in half any lice left on their bodies.

One officer refused to participate in this morning ritual of delousing and more and more lice kept attacking him until his entire body was covered and he finally died. Pharis participated in the detail which took him up the hill to join the others who had died. Pharis couldn't help but notice that every vein over the officer's entire body had holes like needle points where the lice had literally sucked out all of his blood. The officer obviously had suffered from a bad case of "give-up-itis".

During the cold winter months, no one wanted to gather wood for the enemy. When spring arrived, however, carrying wood was much easier, especially when one of the Turks introduced Pharis to a weed that grew wild in Korea. This weed made life a lot easier in the prison camp. Some called it "Texas Loco" weed. Today we call it marijuana, or Mary J. Pharis and his friends started smuggling the plants back to their camp where the experienced Turk showed them how to dry it and smoke it.

One night, Pharis and his friends got under a blanket and started smoking their new-found treasure. Of course, the laughing started and the guards came in and demanded to know what they were laughing about. That just made the guys laugh harder. Confused by the prisoners' actions, the guards started beating them for not answering. The laughing just got louder. When the beatings didn't deter the laughing, the guards must have thought that the prisoners had finally cracked up, gone mad, and could possibly present a physical danger to them. Finally, out of frustration, the guards left them alone with their laughter. It was decided that the guards never suspected what was happening and never realized what a treasure they had right in front of them, growing wild in unlimited amounts. Maybe if the Tiger had found this weed, he wouldn't have had the need to kill for his entertainment. He could have smoked some "pot" and laughed a little, or a lot.

As the weather started to warm, the guards for the first time allowed the prisoners to go to the Yalu River to take a bath. Pharis remembers the water was still frozen in spots but it didn't matter to him. He couldn't pass up the first opportunity to bathe since he had been captured. After all, he had been willing to get into a frozen lake back home when he and his brother Bill had tried to teach those puppies to swim. This wasn't much different.

As the prisoners shed their clothes and caught a glimpse of the bodies of their fellow soldiers, their shocked faces told the story of what had happened to those bodies which had at one time been strong and healthy. Their bodies had transformed into mere skeletons, emaciated bodies, with sore-riddled flesh hanging from the bones, through no fault of their own. Still Pharis and some of the others felt embarrassment and shame as the pictures of their own bodies were reflected in the eyes of the other prisoners. They vowed to steal more food or catch more snakes and frogs.

The death count increased to include another 222 people during their time at Hanjang-ni. As the POW's died, they were stripped of their clothes. After all, they wouldn't need their clothing any more. Only the living needed clothes. The dead were carried to a nearby hill where they were stacked up. No one was allowed to dig graves for them even if they had anything to dig with, which they did not. During the winter, with the temperatures going as low as 50 degrees below zero, the bodies stayed frozen. When spring came, however, the stench of thawing death created a tremendous problem. It was so horrific that the POW's had to be moved to another camp to get away from the smell. Johnnie had to get more paper to write all the names down.

During the first winter in Korea, Pharis had suffered from almost every disease imaginable. Each one threatened to take his life but he was determined to live to see his family and home once again. The prayers from home and his own prayers were still working because, miraculously, he pulled through each disease that had attacked him but not without serious effects.

In late March, the guards ordered the prisoners to move out to find another camp, but Pharis' diseases and wounds had left him too weak to walk. Normally, anyone who couldn't walk on their own was left behind and they would be taken to the Peoples Hospital where they would receive excellent care. Bull! Pharis and the other guys with him knew exactly what that meant. They knew that as soon as the crowd left the camp, Pharis would be shot.

Johnny Eldridge and about twelve others living in the same hut with Pharis told the guards they would carry him. The guards refused to allow that because it would slow everyone down, but Johnny and the others stood their ground. It became a stand-off between the guards and the prisoners. The prisoners told the guards that if Pharis couldn't go, then they would all stay behind with him. The guards became enraged because their orders were being ignored and they couldn't control this small group. The guards pointed their guns at the prisoners and threatened to kill all of them. Pharis' friends still refused to leave him and told the guards to go ahead and shoot. The guards, extremely frustrated, knew they had to get going to catch up with the rest of the prisoners. Finally, the guards agreed to allow the prisoners to carry Pharis until he could manage to walk on his own.

Pharis said that he owes his life to Johnny and the others who stood up for him that day, and to the prayers from home, and to his Lord above. Another miracle.

The prisoners left Hanjang-ni on March 29, 1951, headed to their new camp at Andong. On the way, they had to pass through Chunggang, where the Death March had ended. As they approached the area, the sky filled with American B-29 bombers, the first that had been seen by the prisoners since Pyongyang.

At first, the POW's were excited to see the bombers, but they soon realized that they were standing in the area that was being bombed. Pharis and the other prisoners were petrified that bombs were being dropped on them by their own bombers. They scrambled to find shelter of any kind to protect themselves. Some parts of the river were still frozen where the bombs hit the water. Pharis saw a piece of ice at least 1" thick as big as a house fly over his head. The planes dropped another three or four bombs on a nearby bridge. Pharis thought that to die like this would really be ironic. He had survived everything that the North Koreans and the Tiger had thrown at him and now he could be killed by his own Air Force. Fortunately, only one of our soldiers was wounded.

Pharis said that he and some other POW's received some justice that day when one of our planes strafed the area. One of the bullets hit a North Korean guard whom they called "Rabbit". He was probably the cruelest of all the guards and had taken a great deal of pleasure in beating and torturing Pharis and other POW's. Like everyone else, Rabbit was scurrying around in a panic to find a place to hide. The shrapnel hit Rabbit at the top of his back, traveled south, and exited out of his derriere. Rabbit was screaming from the pain and stumbling around like a mad man until he fell. To his misfortune, Rabbit fell on a stick which pierced his right eye, leaving him blind in that eye.

While no one should have to experience that kind of tragedy, the ones who had been the recipient of his brutality had to smile. What goes around, comes around. Nice shot for our side!

The POW's arrived at their new camp in Andong on March 30, 1951 where they would spend the summer. It was a few miles away, southwest of Chunggang, and once again they were housed in Japanese Army barracks. Pharis remembers that MAJ Dunn constantly walked back and forth from one end to the other of the long buildings, checking on the POW's. Dunn's stature showed his great dignity and character and Pharis felt proud to serve under him.

The North Koreans ordered the POW's to plant a garden at the new location. The garden included a vegetable that looked like lettuce but it was courser. They also planted diecons which looked like carrots but tasted like turnips. Every day Pharis and about six or eight other POW's had the unfortunate duty of cleaning out the latrines and carrying the human waste to fertilize the gardens. They moved the human waste in honey buckets, held by flattened bamboo sticks, just like the one that had killed his Hawaiian friend.

The Tiger had been moved to another location and the soldiers thought that their days would no longer be filled with the fear of being shot at any time, but they were wrong. The Tiger had been replaced with an even more sadistic, evil man who gave them even more reasons to be concerned about their survival. While it was obvious that the Tiger enjoyed killing people, this new man enjoyed seeing them suffer greatly before they died. Pharis remembers seeing this new commander catch rats and set them on fire before turning them loose. Pharis said that he couldn't confirm it because he never saw it, but he had heard others talking about seeing this maniac doing the same to some of the prisoners. It was hard to believe that this little short man who looked like a kid could be so cruel and sadistic. The POW's endured the rule of this evil commander for about six months before he moved to another location.

Eventually the physical treatment improved at Andong, but they were faced with a new kind of abuse. Pharis and the other prisoners were constantly being exposed to anti-American and pro-Communist propaganda lectures and brutal interrogations. The Chinese urged the North Koreans to take advantage of every opportunity to "turn" or "re-educate" their captive audiences. Each morning, both the officers and the enlisted men were herded together into the hundreds of political lectures. They were required to sit for at least four hours at a stretch and were punished with a kick if they were caught not paying attention.

In the summer of 1951, the Chinese realized that the POW's should be allowed to live if their propaganda about "the lenient treatment" was to have any meaning. The conditions in the camp got better and morale improved.

Some of the prisoners started mixing more with the civilian POW's but the North Koreans were afraid that these new friendships could cause them problems. They might conspire to undermine their captors. The guards repeatedly told the military POW's that the civilians were not to be trusted and that they were a bad influence on the military POW's. In an effort to separate the military from the civilians, they moved the civilians to a farmhouse on May 10, 1951.

By that time, the prisoners were feeling better about themselves, morale was up, self-respect had been regained, and most of them had decided that they would survive one way or another. They just had to find more to eat. Pharis remembered his friend, Jack Browning, who could steal and find food better than anyone else. Pharis said, "He was the best scrounger that we had."

In spite of the better treatment and better conditions, another 50 POW's died during the six plus months they stayed in Andong. The diseases that they had contacted and the abuse they had received earlier from the North Koreans had finally caught up with them. Johnnie's list kept getter longer and longer.

Chapter 16

—∞—

News about Pharis

About three weeks after Pharis was captured, we received a telegram from the Army dated August 13, 1950, the first communication that we had received regarding him since his last letter dated June 29, 1950. Until that time, we didn't know that Pharis had been re-assigned to the 24th Division. We all were concerned that we had not received any mail from him in weeks but never dreamed that he had been sent to Korea and put in harm's way.

The telegram read as follows:

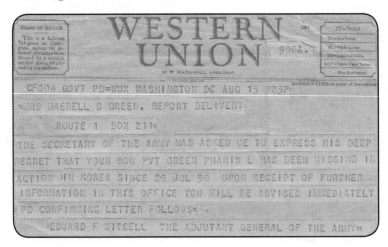

We all feared that the Army was really trying to tell us that Pharis had been killed in Korea, but they didn't have any evidence to support it. They had not found his body. I should say that everyone thought that except Mama. She said, "If Pharis were dead, I would know it. I would feel it in my heart. He is not dead. He's alive somewhere."

Mama had always prayed for Pharis' safety but now the prayers became more intense. I remember hearing her walking the floors all night, every night, praying that God would bring her son home safely to us. She had lost the ability to do anything except pray for Pharis. She seemed to have forgotten that she had a husband and four other children who needed her attention too. Daddy tried to reason with Mama to get her to pull herself together for the sake of the family, especially the younger children, but she couldn't focus on anything but Pharis. Daddy tried to hold the family together as well as he could without the help of Mama, but the whole situation really put a tremendous strain on our once happy home life. Mama and Daddy's marriage also suffered and began to unravel.

The crops had not done well since Pharis had left and the lack of money to provide for the family became a bigger problem. In addition to tending the farm, Daddy took a job as a carpenter and later as a textile worker to try to make ends meet but it still wasn't enough. To help with the finances, my brother Bill quit school and got a job at the local service station during the day. At night, he plowed the fields with Daddy's tractor. My sister Margaret rode along with Bill to keep him company. Boy, they really missed having their older brother around!

Margaret also became a second mother to my brother C. B. and me. It became her responsibility to make sure that he and I were fed and bathed. Years later I teased Margaret about the way she washed us before putting us to bed. She scrubbed our arms and legs with such a vengeance that I wasn't sure there would be any skin left, but I didn't dare mention it to her at the time. Looking back, she must have been frustrated with her new responsibilities. As a beautiful and popular teenager, I'm sure she would much rather have been going out and socializing with her friends.

Sometimes, when Mama and Daddy had to go out at night, Bill had the responsibility of taking care of C. B. and me. One night he and I decided that Bill had a bad attitude about staying at home with us and we didn't like it. We knew that he would rather have been out with his friends but he was stuck with us. It wasn't our fault and Bill just needed to suck it up. C. B. and I decided that he needed an attitude adjustment and we wanted to teach him a lesson. After all, we could handle him; there were two of us and only one of him. We both jumped on him at the same time and proceeded to "beat him up". It was not Bill who received the change of attitude; it was the two of us. Bill spanked both of us and put us to bed. Later he came into the bedroom and told me that he was sorry he had to spank me. That apology solidified our already close relationship and made it even stronger.

Like Pharis, both Bill and Margaret had to grow up long before their time. Like Pharis, both of them made many sacrifices that probably affected them the rest of their lives. Everyone had to do double-duty to pick up the slack while Pharis was gone. C. B. and I were too small to help with the crops or anything else for that matter. I remember watching as my family appeared to be falling apart and realizing that I was helpless to do anything about it. That's a really scary feeling for a small child; seeing it happen with no power to change it.

After we received the news that Pharis was missing in action, Mama never stopped trying to get any information on him that she could find. She insisted that he was alive somewhere. We didn't have a telephone or a television. Those were luxuries that our family couldn't afford. We had to rely on the radio, newspapers, and magazines for any news about the war. In one magazine, Mama found a picture of a soldier standing over some dead bodies. The soldier was standing with his left hand on his hip, a stance that was unique to Pharis. She was convinced that the soldier was her son and even more convinced that he was alive. She constantly wrote the Army and anyone else who had been assigned to either his original unit or his new one.

Soldier in the magazine

On March 13, 1951, we received the second telegram from the Army which was in response to Mama's inquiries about Pharis.

A few days later, we received a letter from the headquarters of the 21st Infantry Regiment, Office of The Commanding Officer, APO 24, again in response to Mama's inquiries about Pharis. The letter confirmed that Pharis had been assigned to the 34th Infantry Regiment, Company "K", which was defending Taejon. The letter stated, *"On the 20th of July, 1950, enemy forces, in great numbers, attacked their positions on the edge of the town. Soon afterwards the town fell into enemy hands. He was last seen that day, with other members of his company, fighting bravely to repel the attack."*

The letter gave the name and address of the only member of Pharis' company who remained with their regiment. The letter was signed by **James J. McCrimmon, WOJG USA, Asst. Personnel Adj.**

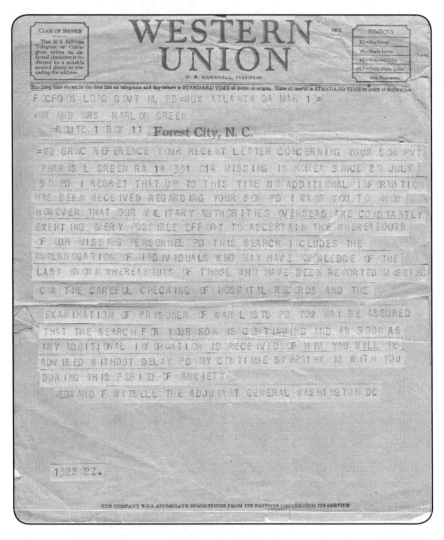

Mama quickly followed up with the name of the soldier in Pharis' regiment and received a letter dated August 23, 1951 from James (Jimmy) Munsey who had been assigned to Pharis' original unit. It had taken a long time for Mama's letter to reach him because he had been transferred several times since he last saw Pharis. Instead of calling him Pharis, Jimmy called him Phil. He said that he and Phil were "such good friends" when they both were in the 7ᵗʰ Division, but he had not heard from Phil since Jimmy left the outfit.

Jimmy told Mama that he himself had been on the boat when they made the landing at the Inchon invasion with some of the 7ᵗʰ Division. He had asked some of the guys if they knew where Phil had been re-assigned. They only knew that he had been transferred to the 24ᵗʰ Division when they came over to Korea. None of them knew what happened after that and said, ***"Only God knows."***

Jimmy promised Mama that if and when he got the chance, he would go to the 24ᵗʰ Division and try to trace Phil from there. He didn't give her much hope of finding out a lot because, as he said, ***"more than likely that (what he found out) won't be much since all the old guys that knew him will probably either be dead or rotated home by now."*** His words didn't get any more encouraging. He wrote, ***"So please try to realize what happened and above all try to forget. I know it must be almost unbearable to lose a loved one in such a way but it's happening every day and there's nothing we can do except face the facts and pray to God that it'll (the war) end soon."***

Mama was already discouraged and depressed about that fact that her son was missing. It seemed that the crying and the praying never stopped. Now she felt that she had just been punched in the face by the butt of the enemy's rifle. She vowed that she would not listen to the words of Jimmy. He didn't know her son as well as he thought he did. She knew Pharis was a fighter who had a strong will to live. He was alive somewhere and she would never give up hope of finding him and bringing him home to his loved ones. The hell with Jimmy's pessimistic words!

Mama received another letter from James dated September 10, 1951. He told her that another guy who was in the 7ᵗʰ Division told him that Phil was sent to Korea around the first of July. The rest of the information that James provided differed from anything Mama had heard so far.

The other guy told James that Phil's unit was ordered to cross some body of water on a raft. He reported that, when Phil was about *"half way across the water, the Chinese unleashed a murderous barrage of machine gun fire that turned the co.'s back and caused an awful lot of casualties and many GI's (were) missing because of a lot of overturned rafts."* The other unnamed guy said that was the last time he saw "Phil or heard of him". Mama still refused to believe that Pharis was dead no matter what anyone said. Mama's crying and praying continued.

Time passed and the Greene family suffered through yet another saddened Christmas without Pharis. No matter how hard everyone tried, the joy of Christmas just wasn't the same as it had been when we all had been together at Christmas.

The tension and frustration between our parents heightened and I witnessed the first "discussion" between them that I had ever heard. Daddy was just as upset and worried about Pharis as Mama but the pain seemed to overwhelm her and she wasn't able to function. He declared that her obsession over Pharis was not fair to the rest of us. She tried to pull herself together but sadly with little success. I hadn't seen her smile since Pharis was reported missing.

On December 30, 1951, we received the third telegram. Before we opened it, no one knew whether it was good news or bad. We didn't know whether Pharis had been found or if he had been found alive. We later learned that the Communists had refused to provide the names of the POW's until December, 1951 when the cease-fire negotiations began.

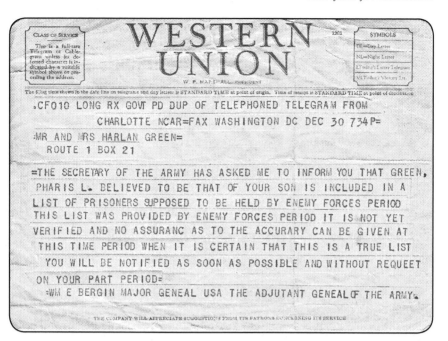

The spirits of the whole family escalated to the point that someone would have thought that Jesus had just returned from the grave. Pharis was alive!! There was screaming and crying and thanking God for sparing Pharis' life. Mama couldn't control her emotions. None of us could. Our prayers had been answered. She had known that her son was alive. She had told everybody that he wasn't dead. She knew that she would have felt it in her heart if he had died. She had kept up with any news about Korea that was available. Mama said that when the UN troops recaptured Taejon and Pharis' body had not been found, she was sure he was alive.

Mama shared with us a dream that she had about Pharis. He was crying and calling for her. She knew he was alive and vowed that she wouldn't let a day go by without a prayer for Pharis. A prayer each day? Try hours and hours of prayers each day, every day. The prayers continued after we received the news that he was alive but now we asked God to bring him home to us safely and in one piece.

Chapter 17

—ᴍᴍ—

China Intervenes and MacArthur is Fired

As the POW's in Pharis' camp focused on surviving, the UN forces continued to drive the North Koreans back north. GEN MacArthur vowed to keep his promise to Truman to end the war in November and have the troops home for Christmas. MacArthur had not, however, counted on the Chinese intervening and entering into the Korean War.

In early July, China's leader Mao created the Northeast Border Defense Army, the NEBDA, and positioned it along the Korean border. It included some of China's best troops and numbered thirty-six divisions, some 700,000 men, seven artillery divisions, and some anti-aircraft units. The North Korean leader Kim had ignored the intelligence warnings about a possible amphibious landing at Inchon and he had paid desperately for it. In late September 1950, after the North Korean army started to retreat north, Mao began to seriously consider an intervention by China. Mao called his troops "volunteers" in order to prevent an all-out war with the Americans. His plans included an advantage of four to one in manpower on the battlefield and a two to one advantage in mortars. He did not envision a long war and asked the Soviet Union for air cover which Stalin had promised. Stalin later reneged on that promise.

The New York Times had reported as early as October, 1950, that between 200,000 and 250,000 Chinese soldiers had mobilized along the Yalu River. The CIA finally admitted in October that the Chinese would enter the war but only for the purpose of defending its power stations along the Yalu River. On November 8th, the CIA further reported that about 35,000 Chinese troops were already in Korea and another 700,000 were waiting on China's border. On November 19th, the Soviet Union's radios broadcasted that the Chinese's intervention into the Korean War was now imminent. MacArthur just wasn't listening. He ignored the intelligence reports, again.

By November 20, 1950, the UN forces had reached the Manchurian border. By November 24th, they held a line that extended from Sodong in the northeast to Hyesanjin on the Yalu River and southwest to Chongju on the Korea Bay. For the time being, their advance north met with very little resistance.

On November 25, 1950, China's leader Mao lost his favorite son, Anquig. He was killed in a bombing raid on Pyongyang. It's not known why Anquig was in that city at that particular time or whether Mao had received the news of his son's death before the next day. Either way, it was obvious that when Mao heard of his son's death, he became more determined to destroy as many of the enemy as he possibly could in reverence of his son. I'm sure that he vowed that he would make the UN forces pay for his son's life. While no one should ever lose a son, Mao had to take some responsibility for the price of a war that he was so deeply involved in. He helped start the war and he paid an extremely high price for it.

On November 26th, as the UN forces crossed the Manchurian border, the Chinese launched their massive counter-attack. The

UN troops had no choice but to retreat. It became one of the most humiliating defeats the US had ever suffered on the battlefield. The plans that the Pentagon in Washington and MacArthur had to "rollback" communism had failed miserably.

As the retreat south by the UN forces steadily increased, the North Koreans and the Chinese troops still displayed their barbaric actions, showing no concern for human lives. On December 1, 1950, the slaughter of over 100 wounded UN troops shocked the world. The wounded had been loaded on litters and were being sent by ambulances, trucks, and jeeps to get medical attention. The Chinese set up a roadblock near Kunu-ri just a few miles northwest of the location where the Sunchon Tunnel Massacre had taken place on October 30th just a little over a month before.

When it became obvious that the UN vehicles would not make it through the roadblock, the officer in charge ordered anyone who could walk to leave the vehicles and try to escape on foot. When the six who ran heard the machine guns blazing, they knew what must be happening. The North Koreans captured the six and as they walked back past the vehicles, they saw the already wounded bodies riddled with bullets. Everyone had been slaughtered.

On December 23, 1950, LTG Walker of the 8th Army who had so bravely protected the Pusan Perimeter from being overrun by the North Koreans, died. Walker had survived all the attacks from the thousands of North Koreans and had helped turn the war around, but he didn't die in battle. He died in a freak jeep wreck when he swerved to miss a UN truck. LTG Matthew Ridgeway, the Army's best officer, replaced Walker. Previously, Ridgeway had made the decision to leave Walker in his position over the 8th Army because he recognized his "bulldog" tenacity. Ridgeway had made the right decision.

The Chinese continued to drive the UN troops south until they recaptured Seoul on January 4, 1951. The UN troops stopped retreating at the 37th parallel in South Korea and resumed their offensive drive again on January 25. The Chinese offered some counterattacks but the UN troops continued their offensive attacks until the UN once again had liberated Seoul on March 18, 1951.

The UN forces continued to advance through South Korea until they reached the 38th parallel the latter part of March, 1951. In two separate press statements made by GEN MacArthur on March 24, 1951, he indicated that the atomic bomb was being considered against China and that we were prepared to take the war across the border into China. MacArthur's announcement that he was prepared to meet the enemy on the battlefield, when Truman was trying to negotiate with the enemy for peace, cut the legs out from under the President.

The government in Washington, Truman, and the United Nations were furious with MacArthur. Once again, MacArthur had spoken without any authority. The President released a statement on March 25 stating that the political issues described by GEN MacArthur on March 24 were beyond his responsibility as a field commander and he was being dealt with by the UN and American governments. The JCS and Truman knew that something had to be done about MacArthur. He was a loose cannon; he was out of control. His reckless and irresponsible words and actions could push the nation into World War III.

MacArthur seemed totally unaware of the consequences of his press statements. On April 5, he informed the JCS of his immediate plans. He planned to advance the 8th Army forward and destroy all enemy troops that were found south of the 38th parallel. He said that he would sit tight for a while and then patrol forward to locate and assess the enemy's position. MacArthur's planned to move forward until victory was won. MacArthur wrote in a letter to Republican Representative Joseph W. Martin, "There is no substitute for victory."

It became obvious that MacArthur was using extremely poor judgment and was not seeing the big picture. He had his own agenda and wasn't about to listen to the JCS, Truman, or the UN. After all, he was the mighty warrior who had led all of them to victory in World War II. He knew what he was doing.

What MacArthur had done was unforgivable and Truman acted in the only way he could. On April 11, 1951, Truman sent MacArthur a personal presidential signal that informed him that he was being replaced as Supreme Commander Allied Powers, Commander in Chief United Nations Command, Commander in Chief Far East, and Commanding General United States Army Far East. He was told to turn over his command immediately to LTG Matthew B. Ridgeway, who had just replaced GEN Walker of the 8th Army the December before. Ridgeway, possibly the military's best leader, was noted for the grenade that he always kept visible on his uniform.

Not everyone agreed with Truman's dismissal of MacArthur. The Republicans in both Houses were furious that the Democratic President Truman had relieved MacArthur of his duties; they had agreed with MacArthur's plans for driving back the enemy. Republican Senator Joe McCarthy from Wisconsin, a lawyer and circuit judge, who opposed anyone whom he suspected of being "un-American", said the MacArthur's dismissal was "perhaps the greatest victory the communists have ever won". Republican Senator Richard Nixon (later President Nixon) said that he intended to introduce a resolution calling on the President to reinstate GEN MacArthur.

On the other hand, the American press, whether Republican of Democrat, basically supported Truman's decision to dismiss MacArthur. They collectively wrote that GEN MacArthur virtually forced his own removal. In war, they wrote, there was no room for a divided command and this was a divided command at its worst. They explained that the majority opinion of the country was to hold a war against communist aggression in the Far East to a point while it prevented communist aggression in Europe. GEN MacArthur had disagreed with that strategy.

For the next six weeks, both the UN forces and the enemy forces engaged in heated battles. Sometimes the UN forces, under the new leadership of LTG Ridgeway, had the enemy retreating and sometimes the enemy had the UN forces retreating.

On the very day that Pharis turned 19 years old, May 17, 1951, his first birthday since he had been in Korea, one of the biggest battles between the UN troops and the Communist Reds started. The day before, 137,000 Chinese and 38,000 North Koreans moved southward where they had been told that great, easily obtained victories laid ahead for them. Shortly after midnight, the hills were alive with the sounds of the Chinese's chanting and singing, the manner of all Chinese at work or on the march. During the night, the UN and South Korean troops heard the sound of the Chinese bugles, a sound that our troops learned to despise. It warned that a fierce and ferocious battle was about to begin. These UN units, however, were better prepared than some had been in the past.

The Reds tried to penetrate the line being held by the South Koreans (ROK's) and the 2nd Division. Even though the ROK's were outnumbered and outgunned, they held their ground for a while, until they were forced to fall back leaving the 2nd Division exposed. By daylight, both sides had fought ferociously leaving them exhausted. The Reds had been hurt badly and started looking for an easier way to penetrate the UN lines.

On May 17th, shortly after dark, the sounds of the Chinese bugles sounded again as the Chinese attacked Hill 800, dubbed Bunker Hill. Communication with the supporting weapons company was poor and our troops were unable to ask for artillery fire and some of the men started to retreat. Some brave officers decided to stop the retreating and vowed that they would take the hill back, no matter what. They reorganized their troops and prepared for battle once again. This time the counterattack was led under extremely heavy mortar fire from their supporting 4.2's, chasing the Chinese off the hill.

During the day, our troops strengthened their defense in preparation for the following night's bugle sounds. This time the officers had a different plan. As the Chinese attacked, the UN officers called for artillery fire which they got. As the Chinese neared the hill again, in just eight minutes, some 2000 rounds of 105mm shell bursts over Bunker Hill, but the Chinese refused to give up. Once the Chinese reached the hill, our troops hit them with everything they had. We fired at least 10,000 rounds of artillery that night. Hardly anyone or anything above ground could have survived.

By launching such a courageous counterattack against the Chinese, the course of the war changed. The Chinese, who had come south singing, expecting an easy victory, had fled back in disorder. The Chinese had lost their initiative and had been hurt beyond recovery. It was estimated that some 65,000 Chinese and North Koreans died under our gunfire during the month of May. It has been called the May Massacre. This time the massacre was in favor of our side. This victory could have been such a wonderful birthday present for Pharis, if only he had known about it at the time, but he didn't. He knows about it now. Happy belated, and I do mean belated, 19th birthday, Pharis.

Chapter 18

—⁓—

Permanent Prison Camp

On October 10, 1951, the enlisted military POW's moved again. They marched until they reached the Yalu River but the river was too deep to walk through the water. They boarded v-boats and moved down river to their new destination, Changsong, which became known as Camp #3. Chinese guards replaced the North Korean guards, taking over the control of the camp. Even though it appeared that the conditions and treatments were better, Camp #3 was always known as the most brutal of all camps. The officers from Pharis' group had been separated from the enlisted men; they took up residence at Camp #2 at Pyoktong, about 100 miles northeast of Changsong. The civilian POW's had been moved to a different location in Andong. The military and the civilian groups did not unite again for the duration of their stay in Korea.

Pharis remembers waking up the first morning before dawn at Camp #3 to go outside for a head count by the Chinese. He looked up into the sky and saw a crescent-shaped moon, with a star that seemed to be attached to the lower tip of the moon. Pharis knew that a star was not connected to the moon; it had to be either in front of it or behind it. Whichever it was, Pharis took this sight as a message from God. He felt God revealed to him that he definitely would see his family and home again one day; he just had to be patient and keep his faith in God. For the first time since he had been captured, Pharis felt comfort with the reassurance that he would be going home.

There wasn't enough housing for all the prisoners at their new location so they had to build huts out of cane or bamboo sticks and straw, interweaving all of it together and packing it with mud. Pharis said he received on-the-job training to build housing, a talent he still possesses if anyone wants that type of home.

By this time, Johnnie's list had grown so large that he had to hide it somewhere in the camp. He couldn't afford to have the Communists discover and confiscate this important information. The families of the prisoners who died would never know what happened to their loved ones. As extra insurance to preserve the list, Johnnie decided to make a duplicate copy and hide one copy in the mud wall and one copy in the ground in his hut. The Reds might find one copy but surely they wouldn't find both copies.

It didn't take the guards long to find the copy in the wall and Johnnie was taken in for interrogation. The Communists thought that Johnnie had made the list to embarrass the Communists' government so they beat him severely. Johnnie kept insisting that the list was for the families back home so they would know what happened to their sons. After a while, he convinced them that he was telling the truth and they let him go. Before he left, they reminded him that they had the power to keep him in North Korea or China for the rest of his life, no matter what the outcome of the war. The Communists told Johnnie that, if he were caught doing anything else that could be interpreted as an embarrassment to their government, he would surely stay under Communist control forever. Johnnie left praying that they would never find the duplicate list which he had hidden in the ground. During the twenty-two months that they spent at Changsong, Johnnie had to add only ten more names to his list. Those deaths were the results of the treatment they received while being held by the North Koreans in the early days of captivity.

Almost every day, all day long, Pharis heard the B-29 bombers splattering the grounds with gunfire all around them. Dog fights occurred every day. Pharis watched as the pilot of an American plane pretended to be hit and the plane started falling to the ground. Just as the enemy pilot was celebrating his victory, the American plane came back behind him and destroyed the enemy plane. What a spectacular sight! Like something that you might see in a Tom Cruise movie. It made Pharis proud to be an American and he had to smile. Score one for the good guys!

Even though the treatment improved at this new camp, every soldier still felt a responsibility to try to escape. Pharis contemplated his plan of escape, knowing that the odds of getting away were totally against him. He knew that he would probably get caught before he reached friendly forces a considerable distance away. He knew that the mountainous terrain would be difficult to maneuver especially considering his poor health. Pharis knew that it would be almost impossible to hide from the enemy because he didn't look like the locals or the enemy. He was just a poor white boy from the country who would stand out like a sore thumb if he tried to escape.

Pharis remembered three other soldiers who had tried to escape that first October in Korea when our military forces were probably just twenty or thirty miles away. Lupe Rodriguez from San Antonio, J.C. Fain from Arkansas, and James Dowling from Georgia tried to make their escape. The three were ill-prepared for the escape but they found a boat which they borrowed and launched it into the water. The boat turned over and they were dumped into the cold water. After wandering around aimlessly for a while, they came upon a Korean home and went in. The man, his wife and son, were eating dinner and the three sat down and joined them. The son slipped out and notified the North Korean Army. When the three POW's saw the enemy, they tried to hide under a hay stack. The North Koreans opened fire and Fain and Dowling, hit with a stray bullet, died on October 15, 1950. One of the bullets hit Rodriguez in the head and he pretended to be dead too. The enemy guards brought the three men back and placed Rodriguez beside a fire. His leg accidentally fell into the fire and he reacted to the pain. The guards realized that he wasn't dead anymore but they were going to make sure that he wished he were. They beat him unmercifully as an example for anyone else who might have the foolish idea of trying to escape. Rodriguez survived the beating, the Death March, and the war. He finally received the Purple Heart in 2008 for his wound.

There had been at least fifty attempts to escape from Camp #3, but none had been successful. Still, one of Pharis' fellow prisoners really believed that he had a chance to escape and bring back help for the others. They all knew the consequences of trying to escape but he was so convinced that he would make it, the others didn't have the hearts to squash his plans. They couldn't stand in his way. After all, maybe he could make it back to our line of defense. Everyone began to help support his decision and started gathering beans for him to eat on his trip. Pharis' friend enjoyed only a week before they brought him back, strung him up, and beat him almost to the point of death, like all the others who had tried to escape. Fortunately, the guards decided not to shoot him like they had done to some of the other would-be escapees.

The Chinese accelerated their efforts to "brainwash" the UN troops, but with little success. The Chinese told them that their families had moved on with their lives and no one back home waited for their return. The Chinese told them that their country had sent them to a war ill-prepared and ill-equipped knowing that the war couldn't be won by the UN forces and didn't care what happened to them. They claimed that no one, not their families nor their country, cared if they lived or died. Every time the Chinese made these stupid statements to Pharis and his friends, they yelled back to the Chinese, "Bullshit!" The efforts for re-educating him and some of the others went on for about three months until the Chinese realized that it was a hopeless cause to keep trying to brainwash this group. The Chinese gave up and went on to others who might not be as stubborn and as loyal to their homelands as Pharis and his friends. The Chinese's propaganda efforts hardened drastically with African Americans, pointing out the suffering that the blacks had endured when they had been slaves to the white man. The remarks didn't get through to many of the blacks. One black man merely responded, "I am not black, I am an American."

Sometimes the Communists tried different forms of punishment for the prisoners who refused to give up military secrets and accept communism. The guards forced the prisoners to dig long, deep ditches and fill numerous sacks with the dirt. Next, they had to take the sacks of dirt to another location and dump it. The following day, they had to retrieve the dumped dirt, take it back to the original ditch and fill it with the same dirt that they had dug up the day before.

During the second winter as a POW, the guards caught Pharis tearing down some of the enemy's anti-American propaganda posters as he often did. As his punishment, the Chinese stripped him of his clothes in thirty degrees below zero weather. They tied him to a pole and doused him with freezing water every 20 minutes for the next six hours. The guards tried to break Pharis' spirit to make him beg them to stop torturing him but Pharis refused to give in. They finally became concerned that they might kill Pharis if they kept this up and they would be reprimanded for taking the punishment too far. They remembered that they needed to keep the prisoners alive if their propaganda was to be accepted around the world.

The guards untied Pharis and took him back inside his hut and threw him on the floor. He was frozen stiff and couldn't move his arms or his legs. All the guys in the hut gathered anything they could find to warm Pharis and covered him with it. They made a circle around him and got as close to him as possible, hugging him and sharing their body heat with him. They all took part in massaging his body to get the blood circulating again. What they did worked. Pharis said that he owed his life to those guys. If it hadn't been for them taking care of him, he would have surely died from exposure. He did survive: another miracle.

When asked about the ordeal, Pharis said that he was just thankful that it didn't happen the previous winter when the temperatures dropped to fifty degrees below zero. In December, 1950, Pharis' friend Jack Browning and another guy stole a rice ball and the guards caught them. The guards stripped them down to their waists and forced them to stand there for what seemed like an eternity but their punishment probably only lasted about thirty minutes. The guards poured ice water on them and then beat them with a tree limb, bringing up blood every time the limb made contact. The pain worsened when the prisoners returned to their hut. Their blood started to circulate when they rubbed their bodies and their joints felt like they were going to explode. Browning survived that ordeal but his friend did not; he died three days later.

Some died from this type of treatment, but not Pharis and not Browning. I believe that, "Anything that doesn't kill you makes you stronger." That experience just made Pharis more determined to survive to be reunited with his family and friends.

Some twenty-one men prisoners betrayed our country and accepted the Communists' propaganda. They thought by agreeing with the Communists, they would receive better treatment and their lifestyles would be improved. Pharis said the first one in his camp to betray America was a man called Cowart but Pharis called him "Coward". Cowart told the Reds things about Pharis and a couple of his friends that made life for them even more miserable. Whether Cowart told the truth or not, he had to keep feeding the Chinese any information to remain valuable to them.

Because of Cowart's snitching, for a period of two weeks at a time, Pharis and two other guys spent their days carrying wood for the North Korean's use. At night, these three spent their time in a large hole, about eight feet deep, used for storing diecons, the vegetables that look like carrots but taste like turnips. The Communists covered the deep hole at night and secured it so the prisoners could not escape. The three soldiers always had uninvited company that wanted to share the diecon holes with them. Rats, at least two feet long, tried to come in from underground holes so the guys stuffed the holes with rocks and kept their feet against the rocks to prevent the rats from entering. Pharis had only seen rats this large at the county fairs. The three men took turns staying awake all night. One of them had to keep his feet against the rocks at all times or all of them would be eaten by the rats. The two guys who slept while the third guy took his turn guarding the holes had to trust that the third one would not fall asleep and allow the rats in. That kind of trust creates a bond that lives on forever.

The three of them knew the story of three other guys who had spent time in some diecon holes at one of the other camps. They had tried to escape from the compound. When the guards found them, they were beaten severely and thrown into the diecon hole. Their brutal beatings left them extremely bloody and too weak to defend themselves against the rats. The blood from their wounds only attracted the rats more and the three of them died in that horrible hole, their flesh eaten off their bones by the rats.

In later years while Pharis was camping at Camp Lakewood in Ocean Lakes, SC, he believed he saw Cowart again. The name on the outside of the lot read "Cowart" and the guy looked just like the one he remembered in the prison camp, just older. Pharis started back to his camper to get his revolver. When his wife realized what he intended to do, she begged him not to do anything drastic. She persuaded him to drop the whole matter because it was in the past and doing anything about it now would only make it worse. Pharis could spend time in another type of prison and it just wasn't worth the consequences.

The prisoners constantly had to scrounge for food. The corn in Korea did not provide sufficient nourishment. The corn reminded Pharis of hominy with the shells still on. If the corn wasn't adequately boiled, the shells would cut the insides of a man. MAJ Dunn had already taught Pharis how to catch snakes and frogs in the rice paddies and he learned to eat them either raw or parched over a fire. Pharis remembered that a toad was poisonous so he only ate the legs. Even the rats weren't safe from becoming food. The rats there grew as large as ground hogs but they were really fast, making it difficult to catch them. The rats had to be caught just right. If not, the rats would take a chunk out of them if the prisoners couldn't get away fast enough. Pharis admitted that he tried rat meat once and only once.

Pharis had learned not to rule out anything for food. The guards found an ox that had died and brought it back to the camp for a feast. They had no intentions of sharing the meat with the POW's but they had no use for the blood from the ox. Pharis retrieved the blood and cooked it. When it was brought to a boil, it turned into a form like Jello. Pharis said blood from an ox tasted like a gourmet dish from one of America's finest restaurants.

One day Pharis and three or four other guys spotted the possibility of obtaining the makings of a gourmet feast. The neighboring farmer's two little pigs had wandered close to their camp. The guys conspired to catch the little pigs but they knew it wouldn't be easy. They had to lure the two pigs over and catch them through a fence before the piglets could get away. It took a lot of patience and determination but, in the end, they had been successful. Now they had to hide the little pigs from the guards or their treasure would be stolen. Their conspiracy paid off; they ate really well for a while.

On one occasion, the guards ordered Pharis and six or eight other guys to grind grain in the mill, pulling the big wheel around like donkeys or oxen. As they surveyed their surroundings, they saw several editable items on the shelves surrounding them. There in plain sight, cow feed, soybean cakes, and oh yes, frozen skinless dog legs filled the shelves. The prisoners grabbed some of the food as payment for their work that day. Pharis said that he enjoyed the taste of dog meat and now understands why the Koreans consider it a delicacy.

Everyone suffered from a lack of food. Pharis remembered that none of the prisoners fought over food because most of them were too weak to fight. A few of the prisoners, however, would kill for food. Others traded their food for cigarettes because of their tobacco addiction.

The Communists were convinced that the UN governments were using germ warfare to destroy them; they just had to find a prisoner or two to collaborate their fears. One day, some US B-29's flew over their prison camp and dropped strips of silver paper or foil to confuse the enemy's radar. The Communists went nuts. They all scattered to get as far away as possible from what they thought had to be part of a germ warfare drop. When nothing happened from the silver strips, the guards got a little braver, approached the foil, and picked it up with sticks and dropped it into a can. Then they rushed over to the hospital and washed their hands in iodine. Some of our soldiers gathered around the silver paper strips, looked down, picked up the strips, put the paper into their mouths, and started chewing. Then they pointed at the guards and started laughing. The guards withdrew hanging their heads.

Another prankster found a dead rat and tied it to a parachute harness and hung it on the front gate. When the Communists saw it, they freaked out. Now they had proof that the UN was trying to kill them with germ warfare! Just look at what it had done to that rat!

Except for the continued propaganda lectures, life became almost boring in the camp and some of the prisoners started to find ways to entertain themselves. They created decks of playing cards from cardboard. Some played checkers and chess. They passed some hand-made balls back and forth and talked about the women back home.

As the situation relaxed a little, some of the POW's started playing tricks on the guards. Sometimes the guys dug deep holes and dropped pieces of paper in them and covered the holes back up. The guards' curiosity got the best of them. They dug up the holes to see what had been written on the pieces of paper. It must have resembled the episodes of Hogan's Heroes when the prisoners played tricks on the guards.

The instigators came up with even more tricks. One day everyone had to report to roll call with a stick which served as the leashes for their invisible dogs. When the roll was called, everyone answered with

"Arf! Arf!" The next day some POW's were given the assignment of riding their invisible motorcycles to roll call, making engine sounds of "booden, booden". Some of those motorcycles didn't make it to roll call without wrecking first. It drove the guards crazy but the POW's knew not to push their fun too far or there would be consequences to pay. Some spent more time than others in the "hole" for implementing these jokes on the guards.

While some messed with the guards, Pharis was not one of them. He had been the recipient of too many beatings and torture to draw more attention to himself. He just tried to stay under the guards' radar, to be invisible. These little undermining pranks the other prisoners played on the guards made him smile, boosting his morale. They helped him get through this miserable life one day at a time but the price was too high for him to participate. He thanked God that he had been born into a family that cherished a good sense of humor. It had certainly come in handy since he had been in Korea.

When Pharis wasn't carrying wood for the Chinese or honey buckets to fertilize the garden, he found some comfort in observing the activities of the animals in the mountains surrounding his camp. He watched as a dog chased a deer up one of the huge mountains. The dog spotted what he thought was going to be his next meal and wasn't about to be deterred by any sharp inclination. It became apparent very quickly that the deer had more talent for climbing these slopes than the dog. As the deer ascended higher and higher, the dog followed. Finally the slopes became too steep for the dog to continue. The dog tumbled backwards off the side of the mountain and landed in the river below. Pharis thought he saw the deer looking down at the dog with a victorious smile on its face.

Pharis seemed to be called on by the Chinese for almost everything. One day, a local fisherman fell overboard in a body of water that was about a mile wide, a part of the Yalu River. The guards ordered Pharis and three or four other guys to dive into the water and rescue the fisherman. They did as they were told and searched for what seemed like an eternity but, in the end, they could only surmise that the strong undercurrent had pulled him under and he didn't survive.

Chapter 19

—⟋Ⱳ⟍—

Cease-fire Negotiations

N o matter how hard they tried, the Communists failed to break through the revitalized divisions of the 8th Army near the 38th parallel and had to concede stalemate. Yakov Malik, the Soviet Ambassador to the UN, called for a cease-fire on June 23, 1951. In the following days, the Chinese radios voiced China's desire for a cease-fire. Even Kim Il Sung, the President of North Korea who started this war, and Peng Teh-huai, commander of the Chinese Volunteers army, agreed to meet and begin armistice discussions.

On July 10, 1951, the Communist and UN delegations met for the first time in the town of Kaesong to open the negotiations. The UN sent five delegates, all military men who were not politicians or diplomats. Vice Admiral C. Turner Joy, age 55, Commander of the US Far East Fleet and the mastermind behind the Inchon landings, was the senior negotiator designated by Ridgeway. Ridgeway had instructed Joy to be "open, honest and dignified". The Communists delegates consisted also of five members, all of whom graduated from Soviet Union universities. Lieutenant General Nam Il, commander of the North Korean army was the senior negotiator for the Reds.

The town of Kaesong was obviously in the hands of the Communists and it became apparent that these meetings would be used for propaganda by the Reds. First, the UN delegates were forced to fly to the meetings under a white flag, an emblem of truce in the States, but the Reds used it as a token of surrender. Next, the Communists refused to allow the UN reporters and cameramen access to the meetings. They claimed that the Reds' reporters and cameramen would take all the pictures and did not need the UN correspondents. The Communists even seated the UN members in lower chairs at the negotiating table, an obvious attempt to intimidate the UN representatives.

The UN delegates attended the meeting armed with very strict guidelines. Their sole purpose: reach an agreement to end the bloodshed and create some means to supervise an armistice. The political and territorial questions regarding Korea could be settled at a later date in a more peaceful environment. The Communists, however, had a different agenda. They demanded that the 38th parallel become the new line of demarcation and that the UN cease all hostilities. Even though numerous requests had been made to allow the International Red Cross to inspect the POW camps, the Communists still refused.

Little did the UN know that the Communists planned to continue the war not only at the negotiating table but also on the battlefield. Ridgeway warned the US government that to sit down with these men and deal with them as civilized people was to ridicule one's own dignity and invite the disaster that their treachery would bring upon them. Ridgeway was right. On the first day of talks with the Communists, sixteen UN men were killed, sixty-four were wounded, and fifteen were missing. It wasn't a good way to start trying to reach an agreement for peace.

By August 22, 1951, the UN delegates realized that the talks had gone nowhere and the Reds had no intentions of reaching any type of agreement. They had prolonged the meetings for six weeks to use every opportunity to promote their propaganda and to give the Communist forces time to regroup and reinforce their formations strongly with artillery.

The UN forces had held their ground under Ridgeway's command. Now that the talks were no longer ongoing, the fighting started again. The UN's next important objective: to control the Hwachon Reservoir which supplied both water and electricity to the region and it became a series of brutal and bloody battles. The areas that dominated the reservoir, named appropriately Heartbreak Ridge and Bloody Ridge, changed hands several times, but on October 14, 1951, the control fell to the US 2nd Division for the last time. It was rather obvious that the tide of the war had turned once again in favor of the UN troops. Our military pressure forced the Communists to reconsider the cease-fire negotiations, but more seriously this time. In early October 1951, the Communists proposed a resumption of negotiations.

The talks began again on October 25, 1951 at the neutral site of Panmunjom. The 8th Army was ordered to desist from any major offensive action and restrict its forces to the defense of their existing line, known as the MLR, main line of resistance. The UN sent the Communists an indication that, if an armistice was signed within thirty days, the existing front could become the permanent line. The UN wanted to imply to the Communists that we had no interest in further territorial gains in Korea.

On November 27, 1951, the Communist negotiator quickly agreed to the proposal and the cease-fire line, the present line of contact, was ratified by both sides. After the cease-fire line was established, Americans and the UN people looked forward to a quick end to the fighting in Korea. The last disagreement between the enemy and the UN that prevented them from reaching an armistice concerned the return of each side's POW's. North Korea and China demanded that all their people being held prisoners be returned to their homeland, whether they wanted to return or not. Truman adamantly disagreed. After World War II, he had witnessed thousands of POW's who had gone back to their homelands in the Soviet Union and Germany, only to be executed or imprisoned for life. Truman and the UN could not in good conscious return the enemy's soldiers back to their deaths or a life time of imprisonment.

A cease-fire agreement may have been established but there was no peace. While the cease-fire meetings had been taking place between July and the end of November, 1951, the UN troops suffered almost 60,000 casualties, more than 22,000 of them Americans. The longest and most frustrating period of the war on the ground had begun, a stalemate between the UN troops and the Communists.

For the next thirty days, the talks continued with empty nothings at Panmunjom as the Communists once again strengthened their battleground positions and sank into their trenches and tunnels in the hillsides. Through December 1951, they created a front of defensive positions for 155 miles from coast to coast across Korea, ranging in depth from 15 to 25 miles. By this time, the Communists were manned with 855,000 men and it became once again obvious that they had been stalling for time while they prepared to set up a line that the UN troops couldn't penetrate. The Communists, well aware of the weariness of the war among the Western democracies, doubted if the UN contingents would tolerate the casualties that would be required to break through their formidable line. The Communists may *not* have been successful in taking over South Korea but they had dug themselves into a position that allowed them to claim a no-lose situation.

If the semi-truce had been a mistake by the UN, their military commander Ridgeway had not been deceived from the beginning. He expressed his beliefs to Washington that he remained certain that they not show any type of weakening will. Ridgeway stated, "With all my conscience I urge that we stand firm."

On May 22, 1952, Vice Admiral Joy, a very patient and tolerant man, expressed his frustration with the Communists and the armistice meetings and admitted that he felt it was hopeless to continue the negotiations due to the attitude of the Communists. Joy resigned his position as the senior negotiator, dejected by his failure to reach a total settlement. He had, however, successfully negotiated all matters but the apparently insoluble one of repatriation. Joy had never surrendered any vital objectives and had attained more than Washington had expected.

MG William K. Harrison who had served as a delegate at Panmunjom for four months replaced Joy. Harrison was a descendent of an old and distinguished Virginia family which included a signer of the Declaration of Independence, Benjamin Harrison, and two presidents, William Henry Harrison (1841) and Benjamin Harrison (1889-1893). The elder Benjamin Harrison was the father of William Henry who was the grandfather of the younger Benjamin. MG Harrison was a quiet Christian man with a happy disposition. When he entered the meeting tent humming and greeting all with a friendly smile, it caught the enemy off guard. Neither Nam Il nor the others were prepared to deal with a man like him. After the first day when nothing was getting accomplished, Harrison called for a four day recess, knowing that our JCS wanted daily meetings for as long as the Communists wished. They reconvened and, after days of arguing, Harrison and his staff left the meeting again leaving the Communists staring after them in disbelief.

Over the next several months, the UN proposed several solutions to the handling of the prisoners who refused to return home voluntarily, but the Communists shot down all of them. Finally on October 8, 1952, almost a year after the cease-fire line was established, a frustrated, now LTG Harrison with the United Nations Command (UNC), made an astounding statement. Harrison announced that no additional proposals would be forthcoming. The proposals that had already been made, however, would remain open. The two sides remained in a deadlock regarding repatriation, a deadlock that would last for almost another six months.

Chapter 20

—◊◊◊—

Letters from Pharis

During his captivity with the North Koreans, Pharis was never allowed to write letters or receive letters from back home. It had been almost six months after the Chinese took control of Camp #3 in October, 1951 that any exchange of letters was allowed. The Chinese screened all incoming and outgoing mail for any hidden messages that would portray the Chinese in any negative way. If they found anything, especially about the way the prisoners were being treated, the Chinese would destroy the letters and they would never reach their destination. His return address always had to be "PFC Pharis L. Greene, RA14331014, North Korea POW Camp #3, % Chinese Peace Committee for World Peace, Peking, China."

Pharis' first letter home was dated March 3, 1952 to "Dearest Toot". He had received his first letters, those from her and his aunt "Munk", since he was captured almost 20 months before. All that time, Pharis had to rely on his own faith and determination to survive without any encouragement or support from his family. That's really a tall order for a 19 year old. He wrote about the mail call, "Honey, I've never in my life been so happy or so nervous, when they called my name. I was shaking all over. I felt almost like crying. You don't know how it felt to hear from someone I've loved so, especially when I hadn't heard from you or the family in so long."

He went on writing about lighter subjects. He called her "Honey" and "Sweetheart" and asked her not to get married until he got back home and asked her about her new boyfriend and about one of his old girlfriends, Edith. He asked her if she received an oil painting of her and a set of silverware that he had asked one of his buddies to forward to the family before he left his original 31st to join the 24th Division to go to Korea. He closed with, "Tell Mom and Dad and the rest of the family hello and I hope to see them soon. Tell everybody to write me. Love, Pharis".

The letter contained nothing alarming but Pharis knew that he had to pretend that everything was fine or the Chinese would destroy the letter and his family would never hear from him. The family had no idea what Pharis had been through since they last heard from him in June, 1950 before he was captured as a prisoner of war. We may never know the full extent of his suffering or his determination to survive.

The next correspondence the family received from Pharis was written on March 11, 1952, the day C.B. turned nine years old. Pharis had made a combination of Mother's Day, Father's Day, and birthday cards for Mama and Daddy with roses and scrolls that he had drawn. He wrote, "Mother, I want to tell you how much I love you and Dad but I just don't know how to start." He wrote that when he received the two letters from Toot and Munk, his morale was raised by about 90%. He asked for pictures of the family and asked that everyone keep praying for him. He said, "Someday God will let us be together again. Love, Pharis".

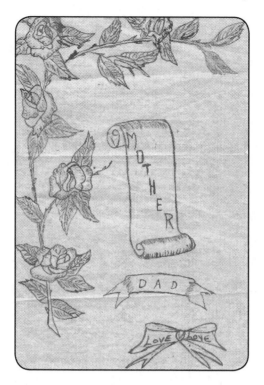

Pharis' next letter dated April 25 expressed his love and concern for the entire family as always. He wrote, "I had a dream of home the other night and it was so real I felt like I had lost my best friend when I woke up and was still here." He remembered that Daddy would be 45 years old in a few days but said that he had forgotten how old I was. He closed with, "Someday I'll be at home with you again and it will be different than it was before I came in the Army." Obviously his time in captivity had given him the opportunity to assess some of his wild and crazy days when he was younger.

The family received three more letters dated June 3, July 17, and July 23, 1952. All were similar when he expressed his love for everyone, tell everyone hello, and asked about everyone's well-being. Pharis always asked that the prayers from home continue and he vowed to keep praying too. He begged for pictures and wrote, "It would be a lot better if I had something to look at that I love as much as I do you." He had forgotten that Bill was now sixteen, not fourteen like he thought. He wrote, "Tell Butch and Helen I said hello and to get ready because we are going to have some fun when I get home." He continued, "May God bless each and everyone."

The family would not hear from Pharis again until the letter he wrote December 4, 1952 was received. He wrote, "Well here it is almost Christmas again and I'm not at home yet. Oh, well, maybe the next one. That's what I said last year." He wished everyone "Merry Christmas and a happy New Year". Again, he expressed the depth of his love for all of them. He said he received pictures of Margaret and didn't recognize her because, "Three years make a lot of difference in a growing girl's life." He appreciated Grandma Dobbins' letter and the 23rd Psalm that she had enclosed; it made him feel good. It was hard to believe Bill was as big as he (Pharis) had been when he joined the Army. So Sis (Helen) had to wait until she was seven before she could start to school because of her birthday being in November. He wrote to tell Grandpa to get ready to go hunting when he got home, tell C. B. to wise up because he had it in for him, and tell Helen hello and Merry Christmas. He closed with, "I'm still praying. Love, Pharis".

Even though Pharis had written the letter on December 4, 1952, the date on the outside of the letter was not postmarked by the Army-Air Force Postal Service until April 11, 1953. The Greene family didn't receive their Christmas wishes from their oldest son until four months after Christmas. It had been another Christmas with all the sadness that comes from not having the entire family together to celebrate such an important day.

Pharis wrote his family again on February 1, 1953. He said that he had received letters from Mama, his aunt Munk, Grandma Dobbins, Grandma Greene, Toot, and his friend Bowman. He had received ten or twelve pictures of the family but didn't recognize any of his siblings until he read the letters because everyone had changed so much. Pharis said that Bill looked to be over 6 ft. tall in his picture and he would surely be a lady's man if Pharis could coach him a little to get him out of his bashfulness. He said he was glad Toot had started back to school and hoped that Bill would too. He didn't want Bill making the same mistakes that he had made "unless he has to". He had messages for everyone who had written him and the little ones who hadn't. "Tell the kids hello for me", he wrote. He closed with, "I'm still praying. Love, Pharis".

Even though he tried to sound chipper in this letter, there seemed to be a bit of sadness that comes from being stuck in the same situation and not moving forward. Pharis wondered if he would ever make it home again.

Pharis remembers writing many more letters than the ones we saved, but they probably didn't make it past the scrutiny of the Chinese eyes.

His letter written on February 1, like the last one, was not postmarked until months later, April 14, 1953. Obviously the delayed mailing of both letters was directly connected to the success or lack thereof of the peace talks.

Chapter 21

—ᴍ—

Eisenhower

In the United States in 1952, a presidential election year, Americans and each political party disagreed about the Korean War. The lack of progress to bring the war to an end frustrated everyone. It seemed that the US could not win a victory, secure an armistice, or even get out of Korea. They were stuck with no solution in sight.

The American people were not willing to accept the number of casualties on the ground required to do whatever it took to win the war. They only agreed to the bombardment of air power. They wanted peace so badly that they weren't willing to do anything to jeopardize their chances of gaining it. Going to war was not a popular decision with the Americans but now that we were there, their attitude was, "Win it or get out!"

Truman's popularity had done a nose dive because of his lack of ability to end the Korean War and he announced that he would not seek reelection in 1952. His successor for the Democratic Party nomination, Adlai Stevenson, had about the same chance of winning the office of President as Truman did.

The Republicans felt that they had been out of the White House far too long. There had not been a Republican President since Herbert Hoover left in 1933, 20 years before. They adopted the philosophy and campaign slogan regarding war of "Never get involved if possible, but once you're in, give 'em hell." They elected General Dwight D. "Ike" Eisenhower as the Republican Party nomination.

In 1933, Eisenhower had served as an aide to GEN Douglas MacArthur who had been appointed Chief of Staff of the United States Army. Eisenhower enjoyed an exemplary military record. By June 1942, at age 51, certain superiors were so impressed with him that they "jumped" him over 366 senior Army officers to be made Commanding General of American forces in Europe. In fact, his popularity with the American people exceeded that of MacArthur. His successful career continued until he retired from the military in 1948 and became President of Columbia University. In December 1950, he was persuaded to return to active duty to serve as the first Supreme Commander of the newly formed North Atlantic Treaty Organization (NATO). Eisenhower resigned his new position in June 1952 to run for the Republican Party nomination. Truman appointed General Matthew Ridgeway to replace him at NATO.

Truman and other Democrats demanded that Eisenhower declare precisely what he proposed to do about the war if he were elected President. Eisenhower answered that his first job as President would be to end the war in Korea. To better serve the American people in pursuit of peace, he said that he would have to assess the situation on the ground where the war was being fought and declared, "I shall go to Korea."

Two weeks later on November 4, 1952, The Republicans took back the White House as Dwight D. Eisenhower would become the 34th President of the United States, with 34.9 million votes compared to 27.3 million votes for Stevenson. He would serve as President for the next eight years.

As President-elect, Eisenhower kept his promise to go to Korea which he did on November 29, 1952. When he arrived under complete secrecy, his son LT John Eisenhower, who was serving in the military was assigned to him as his aide. He spent three days in Korea evaluating the situation. Eisenhower visited a Mobile Army Surgical Hospital (MASH), talked to wounded men, inspected some troops, and traveled to within an earshot of artillery fire. He met with a bitter Syngman Rhee and two of his US Generals, Clark and Van Fleet. He held a press conference and declared that America "will see it through".

GEN Mark Clark, born in Madison Barrack, NY, was the commander of the US Forces in the Far East, and the Supreme Commander of the UN Forces in Korea. Truman appointed Clark to this position on May 7, 1952 to replace Ridgeway when he went to NATO. Clark, now age 54, served as deputy to "Ike" in North Africa and became the youngest three-star general at age 46. He attended West Point and was awarded the Purple Heart in WWII. His son was serving in Korea too.

LTG James Van Fleet, age 59, was now the 8th Army Commander replacing Ridgeway, the position originally held by Walker. Van Fleet served as the former commander of the 2nd Army at Fort Meade, MD. He had served as commander of the Joint Military Aid Group in Greece where he trained and reorganized the army who defeated the communist insurgents in the bloody civil war. His son was also serving in Korea.

When Eisenhower returned from Korea, America had a different kind of attitude. No longer were we as afraid of the Soviets as we had been in 1950. The military program was well advanced and aircraft production was at a postwar high. We had a great deal more confidence in our ability to confront our enemy. Eisenhower stated,

"We face an enemy whom we cannot hope to impress by words, however eloquent, but only by deeds – executed under circumstances of our own choosing."

The discussions of using an atomic bomb to end the stalemate between the UN forces and the enemy once again started. In early January 1953, we developed a nuclear device the size capable of adaptation for artillery. The 280mm atomic cannon could blow any existing fortification out of existence along with the battalions that manned it. It could fire either nuclear or conventional rounds and destroy targets one twenty thousand yards in depth. The JCS began favoring the use of atomic weapons to achieve greater results with less cost and effort. They felt that the policy which restricted the use of atomic weapons in the Far East should be reevaluated. The JCS recommended direct air and naval operations including the use of nuclear weapons. The military shipped the 280mm cannon to the Far East to a storage place close to Korea. Even though the military acted under great secrecy, this information regarding the shipment was allowed to reach the Communists who had no tactical nuclear weapons of their own in 1953.

At a National Security meeting in early February 1953, both Dulles and Eisenhower agreed that there was a stigma that comes with using the atomic bomb. Somehow they had to get past the moral problem with the America people. Eisenhower suggested that the first target be the town of Kaesong, North Korea just north of the 38th parallel, the town where the first negotiations went belly-up and our UN representatives were humiliated. It would be poetic justice.

Dulles, the Secretary of State, sent out messages through diplomatic channels that, if peace were not quickly attained at Panmunjom, the US would begin to bomb north of the Yalu River. The Soviets feared Dulles and thought that he meant business. Dulles was best known for his "brinkmanship" which threatened the use of nuclear weapons, any place and time of the US's choosing in response to Communist aggression. Dulles was willing to go to the brink of a nuclear war and cause massive retaliation. Even the European allies thought Dulles to be reckless and irresponsible

Eisenhower stated in a public announcement that our Navy would no longer be involved in preventing military operations between Formosa (now Taiwan) and the mainland of China. According to China, nationalist guerrillas armed and trained by the CIA raided the mainland of China more than 200 times in the first five months of 1953. The Soviets also realized that it was apparent that the "new sheriff in town", Eisenhower, was willing to use nuclear weapons if the US were denied an honorable exit from Korea. The Communists realized that they had to change their attitude about reaching an armistice and the UN again had hope that peace could be achieved.

It is uncertain whether Eisenhower would have actually used nuclear weapons if the military situation in Korea had not changed, considering the repercussions Eisenhower would face from the American people and the nation's allies. Still, if he had been bluffing, it worked.

Chapter 22

—⚏—

Stalin's Death Changes the War

For months there had been reports of little action on the battlefield or at the negotiating tables in Panmunjom. In the States, the American people thought that this stalemate meant that nothing was going on and the casualties were at a standstill, but that wasn't true. There had not been any full force attacks, just numerous little ones that continually increased the number of wounded and dead soldiers.

On March 5, 1953, something happened that caused a huge change in the war. Joseph Stalin, leader of the Soviet Union, had what appeared to be a stroke. The comrades in his inner circle present when it happened were shocked at his behavior. His body wasn't moving and his eyes were closed. One of the guards made a statement that, "I guess the old boy has bought it this time." Stalin immediately opened his eyes and glared at the guard, but his body was still motionless. The guard became so frightened that Stalin still had the power to reprimand him in his own special way, even from the near grave, he had to leave the room and get out of Stalin's sight. Stalin died soon thereafter.

Pharis remembered the day that Stalin died. The guards in his camp brought huge pictures of Stalin throughout the camp and the prisoners were told that a great leader of the Communists had passed away.

Stalin's successor, Georgi Malenkov, did not share Stalin's thirst for war and did not agree with Stalin's philosophy and involvement in the Korean War. On March 15th, Malenkov told the Fourth Session of the Supreme Soviet that, "At present there is no disputed or unsettled question that could not be settled peacefully on the basis of mutual agreement between the countries concerned. This applies to our relations with all countries, including our relations with the United States. States that are interested in preserving peace can be assured both now and in the future of the Soviet Union's firm policy of peace."

Six days later, the Soviet radios announced that the nine British diplomats and missionaries who had been held captive in North Korea since the beginning of the war would be released. At last, the world thought that peace could be obtained. Things were starting to move forward.

On March 28, 1953, Chinese First Field Army Commander, Peng Teh-huai, and Kim Il Sung agreed to carry out the provisions of the Geneva Convention for the UN's sick and wounded prisoners and return them to the UN officials, a proposal from GEN Clark that had been rejected as recently as February 22nd by the Communists. They also proposed that the peace negotiations begin again. GEN Clark said that he would start the process for exchanging the sick and wounded prisoners but refused to resume peace negotiations until the Communists either presented a constructive package regarding repatriation of the prisoners or accept one of the UN's proposals.

Chinese Foreign Minister, Chou En Lai, issued a statement suggesting a rapid solution to the problem of repatriation proposing that, "Both parties to the negotiations should undertake to repatriate, immediately after the cessation of hostilities, all those prisoners of war in their custody who insist upon repatriation, and to hand over the remaining POW's to a neutral state so as to ensure a just solution to the question of their repatriation."

On April 1, 1953, Malenkov announced that, "The Soviet government expresses its full solidarity with this noble act of the government of the People's Republic of China and the government of the Korean People's Democratic Republic." He went on to say that he had confidence that the proposal would be "correctly understood by the government of the United States".

For two years, both sides had argued over matters that could have been solved in two months had it not been for the lack of trust, the procrastination, the fear, and the lack of understanding shared by both sides. Was peace just a step away or would this proposal also end with a stalemate causing even more casualties on the battlefield? All Americans waited in great anticipation and anxiety.

On April 11, 1953, an agreement was finally completed for an orderly exchange of the sick and wounded POW's and they signed a document stating that, "Repatriation shall commence at Panmunjom not later than ten days after the signing of this agreement." Hopefully this step would be the beginning to getting all of our prisoners back.

The exchange of the wounded and sick, called "Operation Little Switch", was scheduled to begin April 20, 1953. Pharis heard of the exchange and hoped that he would be one of them but obviously his mission was not over as a POW yet. The UN returned over 6,000 Communist prisoners to North Korea and China. As cameras clicked and newsreels ran, the Communists prisoners arrived at the exchange shouting defiance of the UN and stripping themselves of the clothes that the UN had provided them. Many of the Communist prisoners feared that, if they didn't denounce the UN and the treatment that they had received, their homeland comrades would believe that they had been reeducated and agreed with the American way of life now. They would be shot or imprisoned for the rest of the lives. They had to make it clear that they were true Communists.

The number of prisoners received by the UN was a tenth of the number that had been returned to the Communists. The number received totaled only 684 prisoners, 471 ROK's, 64 UN soldiers, and 149 Americans. Seven of these were civilians who had been on the Death March with Pharis until they were separated from him when he went to Camp #3.

The UN prisoners who had been held by the Communists did not arrive at the exchange shouting or even talking. Subdued, they had nothing to say. When a member of the International Red Cross approached one of the released prisoners, he asked him if there was anything he could do to help him. The prisoner replied, "Where were you when we really needed you?" The newly released prisoners did not realize that the Communists had repeatedly refused the Red Cross access to the prison camps. They did not know that the packages that had been dropped by the Red Cross for the prisoners had quickly been snapped up by the guards for their own uses.

For the first time, the world saw just how brutally cruel the UN prisoners had been treated by the Communists. These prisoners who had wounds and disabilities that had gone untreated for years were corroded from starvation and psychologically crippled. These POW's who had once been strong and confident were now mere skeletons of themselves, embarrassed, ashamed, and beaten down. They had witnessed events that no human being should ever see. They had been treated with such brutality that no one should have ever survived. Perhaps it should have been a glorious day, but those being released still had friends being held in the camps who might never see freedom again. These prisoners all shared feelings of sadness and guilt because they were about to see their homelands and others were still exposed to the same starvation and treatment that had been their way of life for years. On their day of release, how could they be happy?

The next day, the radio reports from Peking, China falsely stated that the seven civilian prisoners who had been released from North Korea had thanked their captors for their humane treatment.

Chapter 23

—✺—

Rhee Interferes with Armistice

On April 26, 1953, the peace talks resumed at Panmunjom for the first time since October of the previous year when LTG Harrison announced that he had no additional proposals to make. The Communists presented a six point proposal for ending the POW impasse. Harrison agreed with some of the points but strongly disagreed with other points. The talks once again bogged down. In the first days of May, Harrison returned to the peace talk tables with a counter proposal that was rejected by the Communists the next day as being absolutely unacceptable.

Finally, the US government decided to give the Communists a little encouragement to entice them into reaching an agreement at the peace talk tables. On May 10th, the US Air Force launched one of the most concentrated attacks of the war. In the past, our Air Force planners had rejected the idea of destroying the irrigation dams which would seriously affect the rice crops of North Korea because of humanitarian reasons. Now all gloves were off! This time, the Air Force demolished numerous dikes, dams and reservoirs. On May 15th, reports claimed that "Floodwaters poured forth, leaving a trail of havoc…. Buildings, crops, and irrigation canals were all swept away in the devastating torrent." Pleased with its success, the Air Force continued to bomb anything that would supply the basic necessities to the enemy. It was another miracle that Pharis' Camp #3, located very close to a reservoir, wasn't bombed too.

Secretary of State Dulles sent the Communists a little more incentive to reach an agreement at the peace talk tables. He repeated his previous message to Peking on May 22nd that America would take the battle north of the Yalu River and bomb military sanctuaries if the two sides did not come to terms quickly. The Communists returned to the peace talks three days later with the full understanding that the Eisenhower administration was serious about their threats and Ike was not going to budge on his terms of repatriation. The war continued to cost both North Korea and China a great deal of money as well as many lives and they knew that to continue this war would be futile. They didn't plan, however, to agree to any terms just yet.

Harrison had his orders from Washington before he returned to Panmunjom. The Korean repatriates would be turned over to the Neutral Nations Repatriation Committee – India, Poland, Czechoslovakia, Sweden, and Switzerland. If the Communists failed to agree or provide a basis for further discussions, the negotiations would end and the Communists would suffer the consequences. The bombings would go north of the Yalu River.

Harrison asked that their meeting be held in a closed session where he presented his new plan. After an hour and a half of discussions, General Nam, the chief of staff of the Korean People's Army and the main delegate, made several objections to the plan. He suggested to Harrison that they meet again in four days; Harrison gave him six.

To follow up after the meeting, on May 27, 1953, GEN Mark Clark, the UN commander, sent a strong message to both Kim and Peng urging them to accept the new plan that Harrison had presented. He wrote, "If your government's stated desire for an armistice is in good faith, you are urged to take advantage of the present opportunity." At the end of May 1953, the US was almost certain we were getting closer and closer to an armistice. They had, however, underestimated the determination to stop the armistice of the bitter, covert, and revengeful Syngman Rhee.

Rhee had always dreamed that he would be the one to reunite North and South Korea. He regarded an armistice as a total and completely unsatisfactory conclusion to the war. If an armistice were signed, he would never see his dream come true and he would be forever stuck with just half of Korea to rule. He vowed to stop the armistice at any costs. On May 30th, Rhee wrote Eisenhower expressing his concerns about any armistice arrangements which would allow some of the Chinese to remain in Korea. He said that it would mean a "death sentence for Korea without protest".

On June 4, 1953, Nam had submitted a counter proposal to Harrison, indicating acceptance of the UN's last proposal, with one minor change. Eisenhower advised Rhee that Nam's small change was acceptable to him and that Rhee's government would retain the same territory that they had before the war. Eisenhower stated that he was still committed to the eventual reunification of Korea but only by peaceful means.

Rhee was determined not to back down. In an official government announcement, Rhee outlined to his country the minimum terms for a truce that he had communicated to Eisenhower earlier. Rhee demanded a simultaneous withdrawal of UN and Communist forces throughout North and South Korea. Like that was ever going to happen! On June 7th, Rhee declared martial law in South Korea and recalled all his military officials back home where he issued a proclamation to his people asking for their support for his "life or death" situation. On June 8th, Rhee and GEN Clark reviewed the agreement that the Communists were about to sign and Rhee told Clark that he would never accept the armistice terms as they stood. He said that South Korea would fight on, even if it meant suicide for all of them and he would be the one to lead his troops.

In Washington, the JCS were getting a little nervous over Rhee's adamant refusal to accept the current terms of the armistice. They consulted with James Hausman who dealt with strategic intelligence in Japan and Korea, a man who probably knew Rhee better than anyone. When Hausman was asked if Rhee would sign the armistice, he replied, "No. He will say that you can't do business with Communists or cowards." When Hausman was asked if Rhee would dare set free the anti-Communist North Korean POW's who had refused repatriation to stop the armistice from going forward, he replied, "Yes. He is sure in his mind that the Americans really want him to do it."

Meanwhile, the ROK divisions were being hit hard by the Chinese troops along the 38th parallel. In spite of Hausman's opinion that Rhee would release the anti-Communist North Korean prisoners, Clark didn't dare pull out any UN troops from the combat area for fear that the Communists would advance further. He took the risk that Rhee was bluffing, but he wasn't.

Rhee and only three of his officers knew the details of the covert plan to release the anti-Communists North Koreans from the prison camps. Shortly after midnight on June 18, 1953, some 27,000 prisoners were not only released from the camps but they also managed to disappear into the night and find refuge in friendly homes. By June 22nd, only 9,000 anti-Communists North Korean prisoners remained in captivity. Less than a thousand were recaptured and 65 lost their lives. Rhee and his men had pulled off an amazingly successful coup, an extremely bold move to block an armistice, but with what kind of backlash?

When Eisenhower heard of Rhee's stunt to derail the armistice agreement, he was furious! He sent Rhee a blistering cable warning him that, unless he was prepared to accept the authority of the UN command immediately and irrevocably, to conduct the present hostilities and bring them to a close, it would be necessary to effect another arrangement. Everyone feared that the armistice would not go forward because of Rhee's actions.

Harrison had only heard rumors about Rhee's plot and was shocked at the success of it. He quickly informed Nam of the release of the prisoners, putting all the responsibility on Rhee and his conniving officers. Peking and Nam were certain that the plot was conspired between Rhee and the UN and they verbally attacked the Americans for allowing this to happen. Their attacks were only for show because they too were extremely concerned that the armistice would be delayed.

Eisenhower said that the White House had been put in an embarrassing position, a place where the US could really not swear that it could keep their end of any bargain that they might make with their opponents. Still, he was determined to salvage the situation; he would find a way to go forward with the peace talks. Secretary of State Dulles agreed with Eisenhower and stated that if the Communists wanted a truce as much as he thought they did, they would overlook Rhee's deeds.

The next day, Peng and Kim wrote GEN Clark a letter presenting their concerns over controlling Rhee and his Army. LTG Harrison assured Clark that the UN was ready to sign an armistice and would withdraw all support of South Korea if the ROK Army took any aggressive action following the armistice. Clark relayed the UN's position to the Communists which seemed to satisfy Peng and Kim and the Communists agreed to reopen the peace talks.

On July 10th, the second anniversary of the peace negotiations, the meeting resumed. Eisenhower was compelled to send a watchdog, Asst. Secretary of State Walter Robertson, to control Rhee until an agreement was signed with the Communists. The next day, Rhee made a commitment to Robertson that he wouldn't do anything this time to stop the armistice from going forward. While Rhee agreed that he would not interfere, he wanted something in return, an assurance of a mutual security pact and long-term economic aid.

Rhee had received the attention of the US for over two weeks in order to get Rhee's cooperation and agreement not to interfere again and he believed that his stature had improved dramatically in Asia. He had proven that South Korea was not America's puppet state that everyone had called it. While he was gaining importance concerning the peace talks, his ROK army received one of the heaviest attacks of the war. On July 13th, the Chinese smashed into four ROK divisions causing severe casualties. In fact, during June and July, the UN suffered over 50,000 casualties, most of them members of the ROK army. The Chinese suffered twice as many casualties but their supply of manpower remained inexhaustible.

Finally, on July 27, 1953, at 10:00 AM, both sides entered the building where the armistice was to be signed. Rhee and his representatives were missing. Without conversation from anyone, both sides sat down. Within twelve minutes, the first signatures were finished. This agreement had finally been reached after two years and seventeen days of negotiating, where 18 million words had been exchanged at 575 separate meetings. Three years of heroism, frustration, and bloodshed were finally over, but it would take another twelve hours before the final shots were fired. Once the agreement was signed, the swap of POW's would begin, called Operation Big Switch. The exchange was to begin at 9:00 AM on August 5, 1953, switching 400 POW's each day for the next thirty days.

Chapter 24

—⚶—

Going Home

While Pharis and the other POW's who had *not* been exchanged in Operation Little Switch waited for word that an armistice had been reached, their hopes faded. They weren't sure if they would ever see their homelands again. Then one day hope was revitalized.

The Chinese came into their area and told them that an armistice had been signed and they were going home, but many of the POW's still didn't believe it. About a week later, they received toiletry kits from the International Red Cross, a positive sign that going home could be a reality. Each kit contained a toothbrush, toothpaste, shaving cream, razors, and cigarettes, luxuries that they hadn't seen in over three years. Pharis thought that something was about to happen but did he dare to hope or dream that he was going home? They had heard rumors over the last two years about the peace talks taking place and every time they had been disappointed when an armistice had not been signed. Was this just another one of those times? Would they all be disappointed again?

A few days later, the POW's were told to gather what little they had and get ready to move out. Still, Pharis couldn't really accept the fact that he might be going home after being in captivity for thirty-seven months. While he didn't allow himself to fully believe it, he thought that he would just play along and get prepared to leave this horrible Camp #3 where he had barely survived for almost two years.

Johnnie Johnson realized that he had work to do before he could leave the camp. He had to retrieve his precious second list of information of those who had died during their captivity. It was important that those who weren't going home have a voice. The families deserved to know what happened to their loved ones. Johnnie knew the danger of retrieving his list. He had been warned that, if he did anything else to upset the Reds, he would never be allowed to leave. He knew the guards were standing just outside the door and he would surely be searched before he was allowed to leave. Johnnie had to find a way to get the list back home and then it came to him, the toothpaste tube. Johnnie squeezed all the new toothpaste out and inserted his precious list inside the large-mouthed tube. He didn't think the guards would search the tube but he was still really nervous about it. He couldn't survive the rest of his life in North Korea or China, but he had to get the list out with him.

On August 21, 1953, Mama wrote Pharis a letter even though she believed he would be home soon. She wrote, "Hello Darling, How's Mama's Boy tonight?" She said that she hoped his name had been called and he was on his way home. She wrote, "There's going to be an old time reunion when you get home. Oh, how I'm longing for that day." She reported that Grandpa Dobbins was getting around now and passed on a message to Pharis that he was getting ready to go hunting with him when winter arrived. She told him that they were going to have to "go to picking cotton in a few days". Pharis had always hated picking cotton in the past, but now he could think of nothing he would rather be doing. Mama said that Joe Ford, a POW from the nearby town of Rutherfordton, was on his way home and Daddy had gone to see Joe's family. Mama and Daddy were starving for any information that would link them to their son Pharis, and they hoped to share in the Ford family's happiness. Mama closed with, "Oh Darling, yours (your name) is going to be called soon I know." She signed, "All our love and prayers. Mother & all".

When Daddy visited the Ford family, he learned that Joseph Ford served with Battery B, 15th Field Artillery Battalion, 2nd Infantry Division ("Warrior Division"). Ford's units had helped to defend the Pusan Perimeter and had advanced north to the 38th parallel after the successful landing at Inchon on September 15, 1950. The North Koreans and Chinese troops overran Ford's unit and he was captured on February 13, 1951. He remained a POW for two and a half years until his release on August 13, 1953. They discussed the third POW from Rutherford County who was returning from Korea. Master Sergeant Austin Flack was the first person from the county to be captured on July 14, 1950 and was released on August 19, 1953. Daddy thanked God that his son was one of the fortunate ones who had survived this horrendous experience and was now on his way home. Sadness and compassion for the families who had not received such good news overwhelmed him.

About two weeks after they received the news that an armistice had been signed, Pharis and the other POW's from Camp #3 were loaded onto several trucks with about forty men to each truck. They were being moved to a holding station outside of Panmunjom where they would wait to be repatriated. As the trucks made the long drive across the steep mountains on the very narrow roads, Pharis could hear the rocks breaking off the cliffs by the weight of the trucks. For three or four days, he rode in fear that his truck would tumble down a cliff and he would never make it to his destination and his freedom.

The Communists had set up numerous tents to house the POW's until they were exchanged for the enemy's soldiers. They called it Tent City. When they arrived, our soldiers were instructed to exit the truck, go inside the tents, and remain there until their names were called. Then they would be transported by truck across the bridge to the UN's Freedom Village. It could take a few days or it could take a few weeks before they would make the trip across the bridge to freedom, depending on when each one's name was called. Pharis looked across the bridge and he could see the American flag blowing in the wind. He had never seen such a beautiful, glorious sight in his life. Freedom was just a bridge away.

Pharis did as he was told and started toward the tents. Another POW, however, couldn't control himself. He didn't go into the tents and wait for his name to be called but rather he started screaming and sprinting across the bridge. As he ran for the other side, a Communist guard instinctively raised his rifle and shot the POW in the back. What a waste of human life! If only he had obeyed the enemy's orders. This POW had survived the cold winters, the beatings, the lack of food and water, the diseases, the interrogations, only to meet his death this way. He had been just a bridge away from regaining his freedom. No amount of reprimand for this guard's actions would bring this man back to life.

Pharis went inside one of the tents and waited for his name to be called. With the passing of each day, Pharis wondered when it would be his turn to cross the bridge to freedom. As he heard the names of many others being called, he wondered if this was some kind of bad joke that everyone but him would be allowed to go home. Trucks came and went exchanging prisoners but Pharis' turn was not to come for many days. Each day, Pharis paced and paced as he waited to board the truck that would take him to the "Gate to Freedom". Those days of waiting turned into an eternity and Pharis had to keep reminding himself that God had not brought him through this horrific experience to desert him now. His turn would come; he just had to be patient. It was later determined that the Communists released the POW's in the manner of their good behavior. Those who had not given them much trouble were released first. Those who had *not* been cooperative with the enemy had to wait, and Pharis waited.

While he waited, Pharis tried to occupy himself with other matters. He observed other POW's and tried socializing a little. Another POW who had been captured only about a month before came into the tent. He came in singing "Jambalaya on the Bayou" which had been recorded by Hank Williams, Sr. Pharis and the others gathered around to hear him sing.

> "Goodbye Joe me gotta go me oh my oh
> Me gotta go pole the pirogue down the bayou
> My Yvonne the sweetest one me oh my oh
> Son of a gun we'll have big fun on the bayou
> Jambalaya and a crawfish pie and file gumbo
> Cause tonight I'm gonna see my ma cher amio
> Pick guitar fill fruit jar and be gay-o
> Son of a gun we'll have big fun on the bayou"

Pharis remembers that he had never heard the song before so he surmised that it must have been recorded while he was in the prison camps or shortly before he was captured. It was recorded June 14, 1952.

Another two weeks passed before Pharis finally heard his name called. He was so excited that he thought he might wet his pants.

He quickly boarded a truck that would take him across the bridge to Freedom Village, where the American flag was blowing in the wind. As the truck traveled across the bridge, it seemed to Pharis that it was going at a snail's pace. Why couldn't the driver speed up? Pharis still wasn't sure that all this was real. He thought that he might be dreaming like he had before, only to wake up and realize the Communists still had control over him. As the American flag came closer into Pharis' view, he started to believe that this might really be happening. Tears started to roll down his face. He might just see his family and his homeland again after all. Silently he said, "Mama, I'm coming home."

Pharis and the other POW's were ordered to exit the truck and wait for their name to be called to verify their identification and then they could enter the welcome center. After Pharis's identification was verified, he entered into an area where the US military was waiting for him. An American General greeted Pharis and asked him, "Are you American?" Pharis proudly replied, "Yes Sir!" The General and several other officers chimed in to say, "Welcome home, Soldier. You're safe now." No words had ever been more beautiful.

As the POW's entered through the freedom gate, they were sprayed with some type of chemical to kill the lice and anything else that had hitched a ride on their bodies. They then showered and were given new clothes, probably the first for some of them since they had been captured over three years ago. Afterwards, Pharis was escorted inside the building and offered his first meal of roast beef and potatoes. He didn't believe that his body could handle that kind of food just yet so he declined. Instead, he chose ice cream and coffee. Nothing had ever tasted as good to him in his life, except maybe those little green peas that he loved so much. Perhaps he would try the roast beef and the potatoes the next day. Pharis spent one night at this station. The next day he was seated on a helicopter, with a maximum capacity of

10 people, to fly over the swampy waters to Inchon where he would board a ship headed home. The sicker POW's were flown to Japan for medical treatment.

The stories that were told by the different POW's regarding the trip home vary a great deal. Some said they were interrogated every day for several hours each day. Pharis said he was "debriefed" for about two or three hours on one occasion on the ship. He agreed with the other POW's that those asking the questions knew more about their activities while they were in Korea than they knew themselves. Except for that one time, he was left alone to do whatever he pleased which was absolutely nothing. He was left alone with his joy, his thankfulness, and his dreams of his family and home. The trip took seventeen days which was probably good for him to allow his body to adjust to eating real food again.

Since we didn't have a telephone, word of Pharis' release first came to us from the Forest City Police Department who had heard the news over their radio from Shelby. It was about 11:00 PM and Mama and Daddy were just about ready for bed when the patrol car drove up. I can't imagine how my mother felt when she received the long-awaited news. I just remember that everyone in the family was screaming and crying and rejoicing all at once, but none like my mother. God had answered all those prayers that Mama and all of us had prayed for over three years.

In an interview with the local newspaper the next morning, Mama said, "I cried at first, but I'm entirely too happy to cry now. I didn't get much sleep last night either. Harlan and I sat up with friends, talking, until nearly two this morning, and my husband didn't get to bed until after three." The newspaper article went on to say that Pharis' brothers and sisters were just as excited as their parents. It said that, "Little Helen, the youngest, was little more than a baby when Pharis left almost four years ago. She was perhaps the happiest of all; her big brother hero would be coming home soon."

The Spartanburg Herald

Spartanburg, S. C., Thursday Morning, August 27, 1953

HAPPY FAMILY HEARS NEWS

Mr. and Mrs. Harlon Green and their children are shown shortly after they learned that their son, Pfc. Pharis L. Green, has been released by the Communists. Left to right, ▬▬ Margaret ▬▬, Mr. Green, Mrs. Green and Billy. Seated in front of their parents are the two youngest Greens, C. B. and Mary Helen. The Greens live on Forest City Route 1, where Mr. Green is a farmer and textile worker.

Mama received another telegram dated August 26, 1953, three years and 13 days after she received the first one.

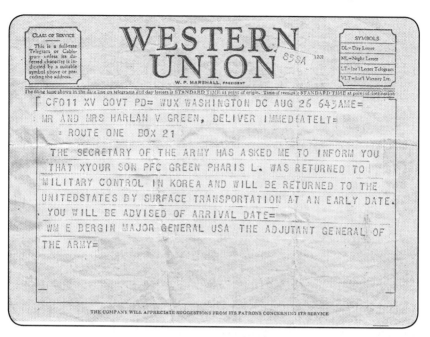

Two days later, Mama received yet another telegram, this one from Pharis.

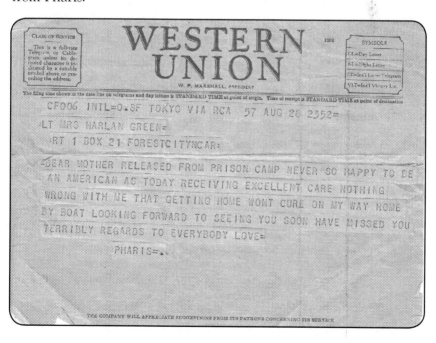

Every time I read Pharis' words in his telegram, "**NEVER SO HAPPY TO BE AN AMERICAN AS TODAY**", I have to stop and cry. Under the same circumstances that Pharis had endured, how many of us could say those words? Many people would have been angry and bitter that the government had put them in that situation, without the means to defend themselves against the enemy. Many would have been resentful that the government had not ended the "police action" at least six months after it had begun, leaving the POW's to be starved, tortured, full of diseases causing health problems for the rest of their lives. How many of us would have still been proud to be an American after all that?

When Pharis reached California, the military detained him a few days to debrief him and basically fatten him up before he saw his family again. He weighed only a little over a hundred lbs. when he arrived in California, a weight still unsuitable for his 5'11" frame.

Pharis flew to Asheville, NC, the closest airport to where he had lived with his family in Rutherford County. After he arrived in Asheville, he did not go straight home to his family. He stayed in Asheville trying to get his false teeth replaced that had been knocked out and broken by one of the North Korean guards. He wanted to look his best and he was embarrassed to see his family again with his front teeth missing. He didn't want to explain to them what had happened. That information would break Mama's heart. When he was told that it would take two weeks to get his new teeth, Pharis decided that was too long to prolong his reunion. He would just have to go home without his teeth. Pharis boarded a bus to Forest City. From there he hired a taxi to take him home to his family.

Without a telephone, we had no way to know the exact date Pharis would return. Luckily both parents were home when Pharis arrived. Everyone was really full of emotions, hugging and kissing and laughing.

Pharis tried to hide his mouth so we wouldn't ask him about his missing teeth. After the initial greeting, Pharis realized that his family wasn't acting like he had envisioned. He didn't realize that the Army had advised Mama and Daddy to treat Pharis as if nothing had happened. They acted as if he had just returned from a short trip to the local store. Pharis was devastated! He thought they hadn't missed him and didn't care that he had returned. He began to wonder why he had fought so hard to stay alive if his return wasn't to be celebrated and they didn't want him back. Everyone soon realized that treating Pharis the way the Army had advised didn't feel right. His return *was* a big deal and the family ignored the advice from the Army. This was no way to welcome their son back! They began to show Pharis all the love, ecstatic joy, and gratitude they felt in their hearts that God had brought him home, and in one piece. Now that's the family Pharis remembered!

Margaret age 18 & Pharis age 21

That first night home, Pharis still couldn't believe he was back with his family. It was just too good to be true and he had a hard time wrapping his mind around it and he wasn't able to sleep. He walked outside to be alone with his thoughts and let his mind get used to being home. The kids had grown so much and Toot and Bill had changed; they had matured. Dad looked a little older and Mama was just as pretty as she had always been.

Daddy was having a hard time sleeping too. He couldn't believe his oldest son had finally come home after months and years of worrying and praying. Daddy went outside to be alone with his thoughts and thank God for the gift that He had given us. When Daddy approached Pharis, Pharis noticed the tears streaming down Daddy's face. He wasn't sure he had ever seen Daddy cry before. Daddy said to Pharis, "Did we do right by you, Son?" Pharis replied, "Of course you did, Dad. I was the one who was determined to join the Army and I have to take responsibility for that decision and the consequences that followed. You and Mama tried to talk me out of it but I wouldn't listen." Pharis' response seemed to take the weight of the world off Daddy's shoulders. He obviously had been feeling that it was his fault Pharis had suffered at the hands of the enemy for over three years. No doubt Daddy had done his share of crying in private over Pharis but this was probably the first time he had allowed anyone to see him do it. Daddy had always been strong even in the worst of times. Now he was revealing his innermost emotions and vulnerability.

Pharis' return from Korea healed all our hearts. The "Prodigal Son", as Pharis often referred to himself, had returned home. Laughter and joy replaced sadness and worry. Mama and Daddy were once again sweethearts, expressing their love, affection, devotion, and respect just as they had done before this horrible nightmare started. We all had

Mama's attention again. Everything in the Greene family's world was right once again. The family was whole again.

The entire Greene family – a few months after Pharis returned home

Soon after Pharis' return, on September 17, 1953, the town of Forest City showed their respect and appreciation for his service in the Korean War. Pharis and the family were given a parade with the entire town coming out to salute their own hero. The Army had awarded him the Purple Heart which he displayed with pride. Forest City and the residents had raised enough money to give him a gold watch and over $500 in cash. When Pharis' back pay finally arrived from the Army for those months that he had been held a prisoner, he promptly spent the money on a new car, for him at least, a 1950 Ford.

It was not until 1988, 35 years after Pharis came home that he received a Prisoner of War Medal from the US government. Pharis said, "When it came, it made me mad. They swept it (the Korean War) under the rug. They didn't want to remember the Korean War."

Mt. Pleasant Baptist Church where we were members honored Pharis on October 25, 1953. In the bulletin it stated, "Our Bulletin today is dedicated to Pharis Greene, returned POW, and all our boys now in the armed forces." The bulletin contained poems which "were composed by a group of prisoners of war in camp with Pharis Greene".

BLOOD ON THE HILLS OF KOREA

There is blood on the hills of Korea,
It's blood of the brave and the true
Where nations they battled together
Under banners of red, white and blue.

As they walked over fields of Korea
To the hills where the enemy lay,
They remembered the Captain's orders
"Those hills must be taken today."

Forward they went into battle,
With faces unsmiling and stern,
For they knew as they climbed the hills,
There were many that would never return.

Some thought of their wives and family,
And some of their sweethearts so fair;
And as they plodded and stumbled
Softly they whispered a prayer.

There's blood on the hills of Korea,
It's blood of the freedom they love;
May their names live in glory forever,
And their souls rest in heaven above.

THE STORY OF SIXTEEN HUNDRED

Not a bugle was heard, not a funeral beat,
Not even a drum sounding retreat,
As over the ice the corpses were hurried
To the hill where all G.I.'s were buried.

Six feet by two feet by one foot deep,
On a Korean hill they lay asleep,
Young and old wondering why
Sixteen hundred had to die.

No little white crosses with their name,
But they are not buried there in shame;
Although they be buried in an unknown grave,
Sixteen hundred faded lights.

A pill, a powder, medicine of any kind,
Or, shall we say, a stronger mind
Could have saved them from yonder hill,
Sixteen hundred lying still.

In their illness tossing and turning,
Most of them knowing there was no returning,
Some went easy, some with pain.
Sixteen hundred died in vain.

When we go home to enjoy our fill,
They are still there on that lonely hill,
Forgotten by some, remembered by most,
Sixteen hundred on their last post.

THE ANSWER

I know that you are curious
About our lives in that strange land
As Prisoners of War in Korea,
But how could you understand?

Many days and nights of misery,
Every hour was filled with dread-
Not many of us are left now
To speak for the many dead.

You ask about our treatment,
Was it good or was it bad?
Our answer is "It's over now
And we are glad."

You ask about our captors-
Did we learn their habits or traits?
Our answer is that we learned one thing,
And that is how to hate.

You ask how we were captured,
If we were wounded, too?
Yes, some of us were wounded,
And what does that mean to you?

We realize your idle interest,
Curiosity and wonder, too.
But even if we tried,
We couldn't explain this to you.

Of death and sickness around us,

Cold and hunger both night and day,
That is the life of a prisoner.
There is nothing more to say.

We hope that your questions are answered-
Please forget that you ever knew
That we were ever prisoners,
Because we want to forget it, too.

At the end of Operation Big Switch, 75,823 Communist prisoners had gone north, 5,640 of them Chinese. The Communists returned 12,773 UN POW's, 3,597 of them American and 7,862 South Korean. There were 22,604 prisoners being held by the UN who were interviewed by the Neutral Nations Repatriation Commission. Only 137 of that number eventually agreed to go back to their homelands. The remaining number settled in South Korea and Formosa, now Taiwan. Of the prisoners held by the Communists, 359 initially declined to go home, 325 of them Korean, twenty-one American, and one Briton.

When the fighting stopped and the numbers were in, it is calculated that 1.3 million Americans served in the Korean War; 33,629 did not return; 105,785 were wounded. Forty-five percent of all the US casualties occurred after the first armistice negotiations began, over two years before it was finally signed. The South Korean Army lost 415,000 and counted 429,000 wounded. It is estimated that over 1.5 million Chinese and North Koreans died. The war in Korea has been called "the century's nastiest little war".

Chapter 25

—∾—

In Search of a Normal Life

Pharis had always been very popular with women. His boyish good looks, his charm, and his sense of humor attracted several women who wanted to be the one he picked when he returned from Korea. His hero status didn't hurt him either. He had seen such horrible things in Korea and he just wanted to replace those memories with happy ones and get on with living. He had met several of Toot's female friends at the parade given for him by the town. They all looked great and he liked all of them but one in particular caught Pharis' eye.

At first, Pharis didn't believe the one named Louise would be interested in a country boy; she seemed too sophisticated. She was a petite, beautiful 18 year old high school senior. Pharis had Toot check out Louise's level of interest and realized that she shared the same attraction to him. They quickly started their courtship and saw each other almost every day and night. After what Pharis had been through, he didn't see any reason to postpone moving forward with his life. One month after they first met, on October 13, 1953, Pharis asked Louise to marry him and she said yes. The next day, he asked for her father's permission who also said yes.

On one occasion when he was going to see Louise, my brother C. B. and I decided to go with him. We knew that if we asked to go, he would say no. We thought we could outsmart Pharis. C.B. and I had quickly forgotten our failed attempt to outsmart Bill when we tried to give him an attitude adjustment. We thought that this time we would be more successful because, after all, we were older and smarter now. We decided to hide behind the driver's seat, thinking that he wouldn't see us. Pharis got into the car and drove to Louise's house. When we arrived, C.B. and I jumped up and shouted, "Surprise!" Pharis pretended to be shocked and implied that he never suspected that we were there, but later we realized that he knew all along. It all ended great. C.B. and I got ice cream out of the deal before he took us back home.

Pharis & Louise at her Senior Prom

Three months after Pharis and Louise met, on December 19, 1953, they were married by our family pastor and friend, Reverend Bain Cooper, and moved into a new house right beside her parents. Still a very young man, Pharis did not realize that he was not only marrying Louise, but he was also marrying her overbearing parents. Louise may have married Pharis, but she never left her parents and never broke the bond in any way with them. Pharis and Louise didn't have privacy, a necessity for newlyweds. Louise and her mother were constantly at each other's house, planning, preparing, and eating all their meals together. Pharis was never given any choices regarding his new married life and was expected to just sit on the sidelines and go along with everything that Louise and her parents wanted him to do. They didn't know Pharis very well and they didn't know the attitude of a POW who had *not* been allowed to make his own decisions for more than three years.

A few months after they married, Pharis was visited by an Army Colonel and two Army Lieutenants. They wanted to know about Cowart, who Pharis referred to as Coward, and his association with the Communists while they were in Korea. Pharis spent the next four hours telling them what he knew about Cowart, that he was the first one to be re-educated through the countless brainwashing sessions and who had become a snitch for the Communists. Cowart had caused many of the POW's to be punished and tortured and had put their lives in danger, including Pharis.

Like a lot of American families, Pharis and Louise wanted to start their family right away. Nine months after they were married, Sondra Louise was born. Two years later, Christopher Pharis was born. Pharis now had the family he had always wanted. His life was normal once again and he could put those terrible years he spent in Korea behind him. His time of imprisonment in Korea and his enemies across the ocean now seemed like a dream. This life with his new family was a reality and he had left the horrible memories and his enemy behind him, or had he?

Pharis felt that he needed to do everything that he could to make up for the time he had lost while he was in Korea. He worked a full time job and went back to school to get his GED and even completed business courses at Howard Business College in Shelby, NC, enabling him to secure higher paying jobs to better support his family. In his introduction to the Employment Security Commission from the Veterans' Administration, it stated that Pharis' physical capacities were limited when it came to heavy lifting, carrying and climbing, jumping, and continuous walking. It further stated that the environmental conditions for Pharis that should be avoided were slippery floors and wet and humid conditions.

In the midst of Pharis' hectic schedule, his new wife decided that she wanted yet another newer, bigger house so each of their young babies could have their own separate bedrooms, instead of sharing a room. So Pharis, trying to be a dutiful husband, began construction on the new house. It was on the same block where they and Louise's parents lived, just a few houses from their other house. Working, going to school, and building a new house took all of Pharis' time, but he still had the responsibility of taking care of the lawn and other chores around the house.

On one occasion, after cutting the grass, Pharis' mother-in-law came over and started screaming at him for not raking up the cut grass blades. She continued with her reprimand by explaining to him what a worthless excuse of a man he was. Pharis hadn't heard this kind of yelling since Korea. He thought that he had been released from prison only to find another kind of prison right here at home. He couldn't take another tour as a prisoner. He wouldn't survive another prison camp.

Pharis started getting away from the unpleasant demands at home as much as he could which wasn't hard because of his obligations at work and school. At the same time, he realized that there were other women who were attracted to him, women who showed more understanding and compassion than Louise had exhibited.

Pharis weighed his life with Louise and her domineering parents who, he realized, would never stop interfering in his marriage. Louise was a good woman but was never strong enough to stand up to her parents on Pharis' behalf. He knew that he would never survive in that life. He imagined what his life would be like in a more laid-back and caring lifestyle in which he, his desires and opinions would be respected. He made the toughest decision that he would ever have to make in his life. He decided to leave Louise, but tragically, that meant leaving his two young children behind too. The children would later express their feelings of abandonment and their lack of understanding of, "Why did he leave us?" Pharis says that, even today, the looks in his young children's eyes as they begged him not to leave still haunts him, especially Sondra's, the older of the two.

Chris, 9 months, Sondra, age 3

Sometime after Pharis moved out of the house, he met an independent woman named Jean who was a couple of years older than Pharis. It was love at first sight! Pharis revealed later that he had a dream about Jean before he ever met her. When he saw her in person, he immediately recognized her as the woman in his dream, his soul mate.

Living together out of wedlock was not well accepted during that era, but Pharis moved in with Jean and her two children anyway. When their divorces were final, they married on March 10, 1961 and Pharis gladly took on the role of step-father to Jean's children, Debbie and Scott

Pharis & Jean in early years

During his second marriage, Pharis took up several hobbies to keep the memories of Korea at bay. He had a workshop with every kind of tool and saw imaginable. He learned to play the electric guitar and became a scuba diver, volunteering to search for dead bodies in the surrounding lakes. Pharis became a ham radio operator and he and

Jean attended meetings all over the country. They raised and showed their award winning Chows. Pharis and his two brothers, Bill and C.B., all bought motorcycles and drove them like maniacs, cleaning out several ditches along the way. I have learned from my research that this recklessness is typical for a former POW. He was probably testing God to see if God was still protecting him like He had done during his days in Korea.

Pharis in his scuba diving suit   **Pharis with his award winning Chow**

When my own son Derek was a teenager, he got involved with the wrong crowd and started getting into trouble. I asked Pharis to take him for a couple of weeks during the summer months to distract him and get him away from his running mates. Pharis agreed to do it. When Derek returned home from Pharis' house, I asked him what they had done for fun, expecting him to report that they had gone swimming or fishing. Instead Derek said, "Well Chris (Pharis's son) would come up to visit and we all would go ride around in the van and shoot road signs." What!? I was absolutely shocked. I had taken my son to Pharis for his help in getting Derek straightened out and he had introduced him to even more dangerous activities. I knew that Jean was always more level headed than Pharis so I asked Derek, "Where was Jean while you were shooting signs?" Derek replied, "She was driving the van."

Pharis & Jean at his amateur ham radio station

Pharis had never attended any of the reunions that Shorty Estabrook had started back in 1970, the same year Daddy died, for the Tiger Death March Survivors. Jean encouraged Pharis to consider it. Maybe seeing some of his old buddies from the prison camps would help him face some of his demons from that era. Pharis finally agreed to attend just one meeting. In August, 1992, they attended their first reunion in Macon, GA. Pharis reunited with many of his old friends who had faced the same challenges that he had during that dreadful time in his life. They reminisced about some of the bad times and laughed about the good times. One of the survivors that Pharis was especially happy to see was Timothy Reza, the young Italian whom he met when he was re-assigned to the 34th Regiment, the one who reminded Pharis of his younger brother, Bill.

Pharis and Reza at reunion in Macon, GA

Pharis was excited to see Jack Browning, the best scavenger of them all, Jack Goodwin and Shorty Estabrook, all friends of his when they were in the prison camps. The bonds that can only come from sharing that kind of ordeal were renewed.

Pharis with Jack Browning and wife

Pharis, Jean and Jack Goodwin

Shorty Estabrook, founder of the "Tiger March" survivors' group

Another one of his friends that warmed Pharis' heart was Johnny Eldridge, one of the ones who refused to leave Pharis behind to be shot by the North Koreans. He told Pharis that he lived in Florida and Pharis should come visit him there, maybe even buy a winter home so they could spend more time together. Pharis was so inspired with the reunion of their friendship that he did just that. In 1993, he and Jean bought a home about two blocks from Johnny and enjoyed every winter there, spending time with Johnny and his wife.

Johnnie Eldridge showing his winnings at FL dog track

The second winter that Pharis and Jean migrated south, I took Mama on her first airplane trip to Tampa to visit them. We stayed for five days, during which Pharis and I decided to build a courtyard in front of his house. He and I really restored the bond between us, working and sweating in the hot sun while convincing Jean and Mama that we needed a constant flow of cold beer coming. Mama had never approved of drinking beer or any other kind of alcohol. She said beer tasted like horse's pee. I'm not sure how she would have known that but I suppose she had her ways of finding out. Anyway, while she may not have approved of drinking beer, she helped keep the supply coming because it was for her son Pharis.

Pharis & Helen building courtyard

The last night that we were in Florida, the courtyard finished, Johnny Eldridge and his wife came over to visit for a final time before Mama and I left. We started talking about their days in Korea and Johnny shared some of the stories about Pharis' being brought into the make-shift hospital where Johnnie was helping take care of the sick. He talked about asking Pharis if he had come in to die and how angry Pharis became. He told me about the time that Pharis wasn't able to walk and he and several others refused to leave him behind, putting their own lives on the line so Pharis wouldn't be shot. As tears rolled down my face, I said to Johnny, "I just want to thank you for saving my brother's life." It was such an emotional moment for me that I had to excuse myself and go inside until I could regain my composure.

No marriage is ever perfect, but Pharis and Jean enjoyed thirty-five years of a passionate, compassionate, caring, loving marriage until her death in 1996. She seemed to understand Pharis and the effect that the Korean War had on his life which many wives of POW's did not. When one POW was asked if his wife understood what he had gone through, he replied, "My *third* one did."

Pharis is one of those rare, wonderful men who chooses to be married and who respects and genuinely cares for the women in his life. When Jean died, he felt that he had lost his best friend and found himself once again alone. His good looks have never left him, or his charm, or his sense of humor, and he found that women were still very much attracted to him. He dated a few women but didn't seem to find the right one, not until he ran into an acquaintance from work whom he had known some 40 years before. Her name is Elizabeth but we call her Libby and she is about 18 years his junior. Did I say that he didn't lose his good looks or his charm? Once again, Pharis found a good woman who clearly adores him. They work on projects around the house together, especially in the yard, and laugh and tease each other a lot. Once again, he has found his soul mate and he married her on April Fools' Day, 2003. Libby is one of the people who has been instrumental in getting Pharis' story told. Like me, she feels that the voices of all the ones who served in Korea need to be heard. They were and are all heroes and should be an inspiration to all of us.

Pharis & Libby

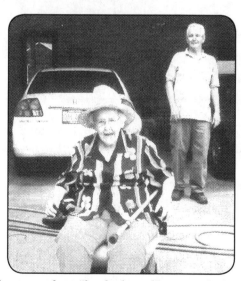

Pharis sending "his little girl" out on her own

—⟋⟋⟍—

We are all thankful for Libby because, when our mother passed away in 2004 at the age of 91, Pharis may have given up if it had not been for her. Pharis and Mama shared a bond so strong that he may have grieved himself to death. Since then we have lost our brother Bill, and sister Margaret, and through it all, Libby has been there for him. Our brother C.B. passed away at the young age of 57 in 2001, so Pharis and I are the only ones left from the Greene family.

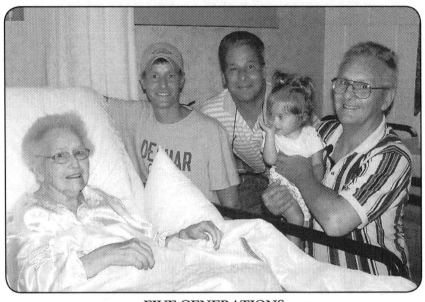

FIVE GENERATIONS
R to L - Pharis, his great granddaughter Macy, son Chris,
grandson Travis, and Mama, age 91 in year 2004

Pharis married three women who loved him with all their hearts. (Louise never remarried after Pharis left.) I believe the old theory that, "If you want to know how a man treats women, look at his relationship with his mother." Pharis and Mama had a bond that we all realized could not be touched by anyone else. None of us were jealous; we understood and accepted it. We other four siblings believed that Mama loved us all equally; she had just loved him longer.

Conclusion

—ⵡ—

Pharis paid a high price for helping fight for America's freedom. He lost 37 months of his life, two years of which were teenage years, while being tortured and starved. He suffers from permanent health problems from his tour and he still has shrapnel in his leg and arm from being shot. He has tormented dreams about his time in North Korea and those experiences come to life anytime he has had to take pain killers for procedures that he has had, such as heart surgery, back surgery, and knee replacements. His first marriage failed in part due to his not being able to be imprisoned again and his relationship with his two children has been strained, especially with his daughter Sondra.

While Pharis paid a high price for his commitment to duty, there have also been rewards. He has the respect and admiration from the American people and his family for his service. The Reds may have taught Pharis to hate while he was a POW. The Reds may have taken a great deal from him, but once he returned home, he realized that they didn't take his honor, his sanity, his love of family, his desire to live, his charm, his sense of curiosity, his humor, nor his heart.

FOUR GENERATIONS – Christmas 2006
L-R, granddaughter Ashley, great-granddaughter Macey,
daughter Sondra, Pharis, son Chris, grandson Travis,
and great-granddaughter Carly

I believe that Pharis' experience made him commit to live every day to the fullest and never take freedom for granted. Since he returned from North Korea, he has always had a hobby of some kind and a burning desire to learn more. He knows a little something about everything. There are not many subjects that can be brought up that he can't contribute some interesting and intelligent comments. Pharis is the most interesting person I know and he has the ability to hold a great conversation for a limitless time. He is and always will be my hero!

Back in the 60's, John F. Kennedy said, "Ask not what your country can do for you, ask what you can do for your country." Some people take that statement literally, like the young men and women who volunteer to leave their families and homes, go to a foreign country and put their lives at risk, all for the sake of fighting for our freedom. As it states on the Korean War Memorial wall, "Freedom is not free." What makes these young people, even as young as 16 and 17, do that? What makes them feel compelled to risk everything to defend our country? I believe it has something to do with strong family and spiritual values.

Webster's dictionary describes "hero" as 1) "a man, often of divine ancestry, who is endowed with great courage and strength, celebrated for bold exploits, and favored by the gods", and 2) "a person noted for feats of courage or nobility of purpose, especially one who has risked or sacrificed his or her life".

If you asked Pharis today how he was able to come home, in one piece, against all odds of survival, he would say, "My Mama prayed me home." If you asked him, knowing now what it would be like and the losses that he has experienced, would he do the same as he did in 1949 when he joined the Army, he'd reply as he always does, *"I'D RE-ENLIST TODAY IF THE ARMY WOULD TAKE ME!"* Now, that's my definition of a HERO!

Pharis sharing sweet moments with our Grandma Greene with whom he also shared a special relationship. She lived to be 105 years young.

Postscript

Today, Pharis and Libby live in the country outside the small town of Grover, NC where I grew up as a teenager. Their house is about a mile from the small Baptist church where I played the piano and my brother C.B. directed the choir. Pharis and Libby sit on their large back porch and look out over a pasture filled with cows. The cows aren't his but the whole scene gives Pharis a feeling of contentment. It must take him back to the time when he was a boy, living on a farm, before he went to Korea.

L to R – son Chris, grandson Travis, great-granddaughters Carly and Macy, granddaughter Ashley, Pharis, Libby, great-grandson Caden, and daughter Sondra, Christmas 2008

Shorty Estabrook now lives in Murrieta, CA with his second wife Marti and continues to plan their Tiger Survivors reunions for the POW's and their families. He also publishes a quarterly newsletter to the members, now totaling about 350 people.

Johnnie Johnson published his list of those who gave their lives in Korea as well as a list of those who returned. You can view his information on the internet under Korean POW's "Johnnie's List". When he completed the list, it contained 496 of those who lost their lives in Korea. Of the 758 prisoners in Pharis' group when the Death March began, only 262 were still alive when the repatriation date came. Johnnie was awarded the Silver Star Medal, the third highest US military medal for valor, for risking his life to provide the families back home information on their loved ones. In 2002, Johnnie was inducted into the Ohio Military Hall of Fame. Gene Scott and Shorty Estabrook were neighbors and good friends. Before he died from cancer in a VA hospital, Gene played in a couple of movies with Dennis Quaid.

L-R Johnnie Johnson & Gene Scott
Both Tiger Survivors

A distinguished MAJ Dunn, now COL Dunn,
celebrated his 97th birthday on September 14, 2008.

Johnny Eldridge, Pharis' friend who lived in Florida, died in 1996, the same year Jean, Pharis' second wife, died.

GEN Mark Clark, Commander of the US Forces in the Far East and Supreme Commander of the UN Forces in Korea, retired from the military and served as President of The Citadel in Charleston, SC from 1954 to 1966. He probably could have gone back to West Point from which he had graduated, but chose The Citadel instead.

Kim Il Sung continued to rule over North Korea until his death in 1994. He was always referred to as the Great Leader. While his people starved, Kim enjoyed five great palaces which no one else dared live in or use. His photos hung everywhere, even on the clothing of the ordinary North Korean people. By 1980, at least 34,000 monuments were created in his honor. His son Kim Jong Il took over the leadership of North Korea when his father died. The son Kim is said to be even more brutal than his father. In the fall of 2008, it is believed that he suffered a stroke. He was reported to be back at his position in the government in a short time although he was not seen until the spring of 2009 when he began his third term as leader of North Korea shortly after launching a controversial rocket aimed at Hawaii. His deceased father still holds the title of "eternal president" of North Korea.

As reported earlier, the Chinese leader Mao lost his favorite son on November 25, 1950 when our forces bombed Pyongyang. It was the day before China entered the war in full force and attacked our military.

It was reported that the Tiger was arrested for selling our troops' rations on the black market. He was tried and given two years in prison. It is believed that he never made it out of prison alive. The North Koreans knew what he did and probably didn't want his actions to ever come up again to embarrass their country any further. It is believed that they probably took care of his death themselves.

In November, 1954, the Chinese returned the remains of the ten POW's who died at Camp #3 at Changsong. It was called Operation Glory.

After the war ended, Cowart who turned Communist and caused Pharis so much grief in Korea went to China where he remained until July, 1955. Cowart, a bed wetter, was not well educated and didn't appear to have many friends. While Cowart lived in China, he and the others who had turned Communists were given a general court martial and a dishonorable discharge by the US government but an appellate court ruled that the soldiers had to be present during the trials and none of them were. The Chinese wanted Cowart to work in a factory but he was lazy and thought that he was a big-shot in China. Since Cowart was no longer of value to the Chinese, they released him to return to the US. Because of the overturned decision from the appellate court regarding his court martial, he did not serve any time in the stockade. Cowart applied for his back pay from the US Army on a timely basis and received it.

It took forty-two years after the armistice was signed on July 27, 1953 before the Korean War Veterans Memorial was completed and dedicated in Washington, D.C. Congress authorized the memorial in 1986, and President Reagan signed the measure into law, but it was another six years before Washington's fine arts and planning commissions approved the design. The original budget was set at $5 million but swelled to $18 million. On June 14, 1992, President Bush (the father) broke ground for the memorial on a 2.2 acre plot of a former marshland at the foot of the Lincoln Memorial. In the middle of the monument stand 19 sculptures, each more than seven feet tall, of men clad in ponchos and equipped for battle. The sculptures represent the different military services and their faces convey the emotions of the war. On one side of the 164-foot granite wall, the faces of more than 2500 veterans are carved. These images were taken from photos in military archives and show an ethnically diverse group of people who served in all capacities, from truck driver to pilot to nurse. On July 27, 1995, President Clinton led the dedication with South Korean President KimYoung Sam and ambassadors from all twenty-one nations who supported the UN's resolution opposing North Korean's invasion of South Korean in 1950.

The memorial reports that 1.5 million Americans fought in the Korean War; 103,284 were wounded; 52,248 were killed; another 8,177 were missing in action.

"FREEDOM IS NOT FREE"

Left, the impressive column of 19 larger-than-life stainless steel statues. At right below, DAV Department of the District of Columbia volunteer James F. Carter distributes some of the information available to visitors at the DAV booth.

KOREA : Remembering Veterans of the 'Forgotten War'

Pharis & Libby at historical site in St. Augustine, FL

Pharis at Korean Monument Wall

GOD BLESS AMERICA
AND GOD BLESS OUR MILITARY

Pharis Greene, a true American Patriot

"TIGER SURVIVORS"

SELECTED BIBLIOGRAPHY

—ιιι—

BOOKS

Avery, Pat McGrath. *They Came Home*. Branson Creek Press, 2004

Brady, James. *The Coldest War*. St. Martin's Griffin, 2000

Carlson, Lewis H. *Remembered Prisoners of a Forgotten War*. St. Martin's Griffin, 2002

Davis, Anita Price, and Walker, James M. *Rutherfordton County in the Korean War*. History Press, 2006

Fehrenbach, T. R., *This Kind of War*. Potomac Books, Inc., 1994

Goldstein, Donald M., and Maihafer, Harry J. *The Korean War*. Potomac Books, Inc., 2000

Granfield, Linda. *I Remember Korea*. Clarion Books, 2003

Halberstam, David. *The Coldest War*. Hyperion Books, 2007

Hastings, Max. *The Korean War*. Simon & Schuster, 1987

Kaufman, Burton L. *Korean War: Challenges in Crisis, Credibility, and Command*. Temple University Press, 1986

Se Hee Oh. *Stalag 65.* Artwork Publications, LLC, 2001

Smith, William W. *A Moment in Time.* Gazelle Press, 2008

Toland, John. Inmortal Combat: Kotrs 1950-1953. William Morrow, 1991

VIDEO DOCUMENTARY

Korea: The Forgotten War (Timeless Media Group, 2007)

WEBSITES

www.Koreanwarproject.org

www.koreanwarpowmia.net/Reports/Tiger.htm (Johnnie's List)